The Seven Day Authors Guide To Amazon Ads

Your Step-by-Step Guide To Launching, Optimizing and Scaling Amazon Ads To Reach More Readers and Sell More Books

Matthew J Holmes

Visual8 Publishing

Contents

The Morning ACOS For Authors

Amazon Ads are ever-evolving, so if you want to keep up to date with the latest tips, tactics, strategies, and insights, then my FREE daily-ish emails are where you need to be.

www.matthewjholmes.com/acos

You'll get the TRUTH about running Amazon Ads that convert and don't require you to stare at spreadsheets, data, and numbers for two or more hours per day.

I manage Amazon Ads for authors every single day; I learn something new every single day. And if you join *Amazon Ads Daily*, you'll be the first to hear about what's working, what's not working, what I'm learning, what I'm testing, case studies, and so much more.

Sign up to *The Morning ACOS For Authors* for FREE on the link below:

www.matthewjholmes.com/acos

Oh, and you'll also receive my Amazon Ads Toolkit as soon as you sign up.

Inside the Amazon Ads Toolkit you will find:

- The Amazon Ads Tracking Tool (to help you track the most important Amazon Ads metrics)
- The Amazon Ads Targeting Tool (to help you plan out your Amazon Ads targeting)

Start reaching more readers, selling more books, earning more royalties, and building a thriving career as an author ...

Introduction

S ince writing and publishing the first edition of *The 7-Day Authors Guide To Amazon Ads* in 2021, a lot has changed; not only with the platform itself but also with what works and doesn't work with Amazon Ads.

My knowledge has expanded, I've seen many more Amazon Ads accounts and campaigns, I've run lots of different tests and experiments, so I felt that 2022 was the time for a BIG update to the content of this book.

This is a revised (98% completely rewritten, in fact) version of the original book that is bang up to date and shares *exactly* how I start, optimize and scale Amazon Ads on a daily basis for my author clients.

I will walk you through the exact systems, as well as the daily, weekly, and monthly processes I use when managing Amazon Ads, taking client accounts from hundreds if not thousands of dollars in wasted ad spend and inefficient targeting, to accounts that are generating profitable and sustainable growth for the long-term.

Why Amazon Ads?

Amazon is the largest online retailer on the planet, particularly when it comes to books. It offers an unbelievable opportunity for authors to position their books in front of their ideal readers.

However, thousands of new books are published on Amazon every single month. And the days of 100% *organic* visibility (i.e., Amazon selling your books for you) are a long and distant memory. Like it or not, Amazon is now very much a pay-to-pay platform.

It's not all bad news though ...

Organic visibility is still very much a *thing* and entirely possible; you just need to tickle the Amazon algorithm (the inner workings of Amazon that decides how much visibility your book is going to receive) enough for them to take notice of your books and provide you with that coveted organic visibility and, ultimately, organic sales too.

One way to achieve that is through Amazon Advertising; more commonly known as Amazon Ads.

It can be oh so tempting to dive into Amazon Ads, launch a campaign, and hope for the best. Bad move. You need a plan of action, a roadmap, a destination; ultimately, you need a strategy for your books and your author career as a whole.

Some authors launch Amazon Ads without a strategy and a plan, the campaigns fail, and so they decide Amazon Ads don't work and give up.

Maybe this scenario sounds familiar to you? If so, as you're reading this book, perhaps you've had a change of heart, in which case, thank you for taking the time to invest in learning a new skill and deciding to pursue Amazon Ads once more.

I know learning a new skill can be daunting, but that's because it's outside of our comfort zone. However, it's outside of our comfort zone that we achieve the most growth in our lives, so stick with it and keep learning; the time you spend now will pay you dividends in the future.

Amazon Ads is a skill in and of itself, and I'm not going to beat around the bush; it will take time to master, and there will be a good amount of testing required. So please don't get disheartened or throw in the towel if you're not achieving the results you're looking for after a month.

Realistically, you're looking at three to six months, minimum, before you start gaining some serious traction with your Amazon Ads.

Yes, you can see results much quicker than that if you have money to throw at your ads, because Amazon Ads is all about collecting data and making decisions on that data. The more you spend, the more data you can collect.

If you're starting slow with small amounts of ad spend, which is what I recommend when you're brand new to Amazon Ads, then it's going to take time to collect the data, and you will need to master the art of *patience*.

The results will come, I promise you that; but think of Amazon Ads as a marathon, not a sprint – you're playing the long game.

My whole premise for this book is to take you from where you are now with your current understanding and knowledge of Amazon Ads (which could be nothing at all, a little, or a lot) through to truly understanding the fundamentals of this incredibly powerful advertising platform.

To accomplish this, I've written the book in sequential order, from Day 1 all the way through to Day 7, with each new day building on the previous one.

I've also provided an *Action Step* for you to complete at the end of each day that will help you implement everything you're learning throughout the book, including launching your first Amazon Ads campaigns.

Learning on its own is fantastic, don't get me wrong, but without implementing what you've learned, you're not going to move the needle in your author career, which is why these Action Steps are so critical for you to complete.

You may decide to read the book cover-to-cover first, without completing the Action Steps, and then come back, read the book again, and this time implement each of the Action Steps.

Commit to whichever method of reading and *action-taking* works for you.

And. in just seven days from now, you can have more confidence in running Amazon Ads, as well as understanding the step-by-step process of building your ads, reviewing the data, and optimizing your ads for maximum profits.

As you'll soon learn, it takes a lot longer than seven days to master Amazon Ads and generate statistically significant data. However, what you learn over the next seven days will set you up for success and build the foundation you need to achieve the results you are looking for.

Without further ado, let's dive into things, starting with Day 1 ... *Amazon Ads Foundations*.

Day 1

Amazon Ads Foundations

B efore we dive into the ins and outs of Amazon Ads, we first need to make sure that everything you do is built on a solid foundation.

You wouldn't build a house on a bed of straw and sticks; you would build it on a rock-solid foundation that would stand the test of time. That's exactly what you need in place before spending a dime on Amazon Ads.

Let's dive in and build that foundation of yours ...

Chapter One

Playing the Long Game

I f you're in this world of being or becoming an author for the long-term, then playing the long game with Amazon Ads shouldn't be an issue for you.

You wouldn't go to the gym, pump out a few push-ups, a handful of sit-ups and a five-minute blast on the treadmill, and expect to walk out of there looking as ripped as a lifeguard out of the hit '90s TV show *Baywatch*.

The same is true of Amazon Ads.

Amazon Ads is all about collecting data and making decisions on that data. I'll be walking you through the data side of Amazon Ads in multiple chapters throughout this book; but for now, please be realistic with your expectations up front and don't expect overnight success from your first Amazon Ads.

As I briefly mentioned in the introduction, if there's one skill you need going into Amazon Ads, it is *patience*.

Without patience, you will likely find yourself taking part in the catastrophic habit of *tinkering* with campaigns every single day. Tempting as it may be when things don't appear to be working with your Amazon Ads, this is a fatal mistake that I have fallen victim to in the past. Messing with campaigns day in, day out, can seriously destroy any momentum you've built up with them.

Unless there's a serious issue with a campaign, let things be and trust in the process I'll be walking you through in this book.

Amazon Ads are not a "set-it-and-forget-it" solution that will transform your sales from non-existent to instant best seller in 24 hours. They require ongoing care, attention, and nurturing. There will also be a lot of testing you'll need to do in order to find what works for *your* books. Believe it or not, there is no "one-size-fits-all" approach with Amazon Ads. Every book is different and, therefore, every Amazon Ads campaign is different.

Don't worry though ...

Amazon Ads do not require you to slave away in front of your computer for eight hours a day, running through reams of data! You can achieve fantastic results by spending as little as an hour or two per week refining, optimizing, and scaling your Amazon Ads.

If you're spending hundreds of dollars per day on Amazon Ads, then you're looking at three to five hours per week of management time, purely because there is more data to look at.

Yes, Amazon Ads requires money, and it requires time. Don't think of the time and money you're putting into Amazon Ads as an *expense* though; think of it as an *investment*.

The *time* you invest learning Amazon Ads is invaluable and will be so for many years to come.

The *money* you spend on Amazon Ads will buy you data that you can use to scale up what works and cut back on what doesn't work, resulting in more profitable ads and reaching a bigger audience of potential readers.

As with any form of marketing, Amazon Ads form just one slice of the pie. There are multiple other activities you could and, to be honest, should partake in, to mitigate risk. These include:

- Facebook Ads
- BookBub Ads
- Promo sites
- Newsletter swaps
- Public relations (PR)

If you are relying 100% on Amazon Ads, or any one marketing channel for that matter, you are leaving yourself extremely vulnerable.

Financial experts invest in multiple different stocks, shares, funds, bonds, etc, to mitigate the risk of one or more of their assets not performing.

I'm not saying to spread yourself so thin with marketing that you have little to no time to write your books. What I am saying, though, is to build a solid foundation for the future, start working towards being laser-focused on two or three marketing or advertising channels and go all in on those. One of them could be Amazon Ads, the other could be Facebook Ads, for example.

If this is your first taste of advertising books, pick one advertising channel to begin with, focus on it for three to six months, then, when you have that one ticking along, add a second advertising channel into the mix. This way, you're not going to overwhelm yourself and end up in a state of "paralysis by analysis" by trying to take on too much, too soon, likely leading you to taking no action at all.

That's going to wrap up this chapter about playing the long game. Next, we're going to be looking at what Amazon Ads actually are; in particular, the formats, where they appear, and how you can influence their performance.

Chapter Two

Are Amazon Ads Really Necessary?

Back in the golden age of Amazon Kindle (circa 2010/2011), as an author, you could upload your book and start seeing sales within a matter of days without any form of advertising.

Unfortunately, those days have long since evaporated.

Whilst the Amazon algorithm does still help to sell books organically (i.e., without paying for advertising), its effects are far more restricted than they once were.

However, it's important to state that the Amazon algorithm is *not* your enemy. In fact, if you work *with* it rather than *against* it, you can still see fantastic results with your organic sales. But it's going to require time and money in order for the algorithm to take notice of your book(s).

Whilst it's difficult to know the exact number of books (and eBooks) for sale on Amazon, as this is data that Amazon keeps very close to its chest, it's safe to say that it runs into the tens of millions – and that figure keeps rising, with hundreds if not thousands of new titles being released on Amazon every single day.

If you rely solely on Amazon's algorithm alone to sell your book, you're going to be disappointed with the results. You need to tickle the algorithm by generating sales and then, and only then, will the algorithm notice your books and give you a helping hand to sell more.

Amazon is a business that needs to make money. If your book will not make Amazon money, then they will not help *you* make money.

There are many ways you can tickle the Amazon algorithm, but one of the most effective, in my experience and opinion, is Amazon Ads.

Yes, you could argue that Amazon is going in a similar direction to Facebook by becoming a "pay-to-play" platform.

However, your time is better spent working with the quirky nature of Amazon Ads and the Amazon algorithm, rather than trying to find hacks and back doors to achieve the results you're looking for.

You could spend time on other forms of marketing, such as content marketing or social media marketing, to promote your books and boycott any form of advertising whatsoever. And whilst this route *can* help to sell more books, unless you're an A-list celebrity or have a huge following on Instagram, Twitter, or YouTube, it's going to be a slow-burn, potentially taking months, even years, before you see the compounded effects of all the time you've put into these activities.

Personally, when it comes to deciding whether to invest time or money into selling more books, I opt for money, as it offers far greater leverage.

Time is precious and finite. Money is infinite, and we can always make more. Personally, I prefer to leverage my time as effectively as possible on activities that can generate the maximum return on investment, which, for most authors, is going to be writing more books.

Ok, I've stepped off my soapbox! Where were we? Ah yes ...

Amazon is a monster of a retail giant. If you find a loophole, Amazon won't be far behind and they'll close it off.

So, in my opinion, just work with them, and it will be a win-win for you *and* for Amazon.

A win for Amazon is revenue, but also, customer experience and customer satisfaction, which is at the heart of everything they do. This is why ***relevance*** is going to be a core theme throughout this book, and should also be ever-present when you are working with Amazon Ads.

For you, as an author, here's what winning could look like:

- Sales
- Page reads (if your books are in Kindle Unlimited)
- Brand awareness
- Series read-through/Sell-through
- Increased backlist sales
- Email subscribers
- Leads
- Increased royalties and profits
- Boost in sales ranking (and therefore organic sales)
- Showing up in also-boughts
- Reaching readers who are in a purchasing mindset

Before I wrap up this chapter, here is an ideal sequence of events that will help you sell more books and achieve your goals. Keep this in mind throughout reading this book, but also when you're running your own Amazon Ads:

1. You launch a campaign that resonates with your ideal readers.
2. Your book shows up in front of your ideal reader.
3. The book cover, title, subtitle, price and ad copy pique the reader's interest.
4. The reader clicks on your ad and arrives on your book product page.
5. They read the description, perhaps check out some reviews, take a peek at the 'look inside' of your book and decide to buy … or maybe they don't buy …
6. If the latter is true, all is not lost … you could have another chance to sell your book to this reader, as Amazon *may* send out an email and, this time, perhaps they decide to buy it.
7. If people buy your book, whether that's directly through your ad the first time they click it, or perhaps when Amazon reminds them of your book via

email, Amazon sees your ad and book as relevant and they start to serve it even more – they could also reduce the cost you pay for your ads too!

8. And if readers love the first book they buy from you, chances are that they will start consuming your other books too; this could be later books in this series, another series you've written, or other stand-alone books in your catalog.

To answer the title of this chapter, "Are Amazon Ads Really Necessary?" with the competitive landscape that is Amazon, it's a resounding "yes!"

Ready to get the ball rolling? Let's move on ...

Chapter Three

Where Do Amazon Ads Appear?

Y ou're reading this book, so I'm assuming that you already have a general idea of what Amazon Ads are. If you don't, that's ok too.

In a nutshell, Amazon Ads allows you, as the author, to position your books in front of your ideal readers on the Amazon bookstore, and you pay Amazon for the privilege of being able to do so.

A little more specifically, Amazon Ads offers the opportunity to showcase your books on product pages and search results.

There are three main Amazon Ads formats available to authors:

- Sponsored Product ads
- Sponsored Brands ads
- Lockscreen ads

Let's kick things off, then, with sponsored product ads, which are the option I recommend you focus on if you are brand new to Amazon Ads.

Having said this, even when you are a seasoned Amazon Ads professional, sponsored products ads will generally make up around 80% of your Amazon Ads account, so it's safe to say that this ad format is going to play a huge role in your Amazon Ads success.

Sponsored Products Ads

Sponsored products ads can appear on search results pages and product pages, as you can see from the examples below.

Fig. 3.1: An example of a sponsored product ad in search results

Fig. 3.2: An example of a sponsored product ad on a product page

They have been aesthetically designed to look as close to an organic listing as possible; by that, I mean a book that isn't being advertised with Amazon Ads.

Moving on to the targeting options available with sponsored product ads, you have a choice of four:

- Automatic targeting
- Keyword targeting
- Product (ASIN) targeting
- Category targeting

We'll be diving much deeper into each of these on Days 3 and 4 of this book.

Sponsored Brands Ads

At the time of writing, sponsored brands ads appear at the top of the Amazon search results, as well as lower down the search results pages, and display three of your books that readers can click on individually to take them to a particular book's product page.

Fig. 3.3: An example of a sponsored brands ad at the top of the search results

Alternatively, by clicking the "Shop [AUTHOR NAME] Books" text at the top of the sponsored brands ad, readers will be taken to a dedicated landing page with a collection of the author's books.

Immerse Yourself In Our Dark and Forgotten Past

Fig. 3.4: An example of a sponsored brands ad landing page

Amazon automatically creates this landing page for you when you launch your sponsored brands campaign. Sponsored brands ads are an amazing way to advertise a series of books and introduce readers to multiple books in your backlist.

Even though just three books are viewable in the ad itself on the search results page, you can add many more; all of which will be shown (and available to purchase) on this special landing page created by Amazon. So, if you have a 20-book series, for example, you can add all 20 books to your sponsored brands ads.

Positioning your books at the top of the search results for relevant search terms with sponsored brands ads is, I'm sure you would agree, a prominent piece of real estate in the Amazon ecosystem. However, keep in mind that you will need at least three books in your KDP account in order to run sponsored brands ads.

In terms of targeting for sponsored brands ads, you have the following options available:

- Keyword targeting
- Product (ASIN) targeting
- Category targeting

With the prominent placement of sponsored brands ads, you are likely to see a high CTR (click-through rate) with these types of ads.

They are generally more expensive than sponsored products ads, but with a more prominent placement and, in most cases, a higher conversion rate (i.e., more sales), the results outweigh the costs.

Lockscreen Ads

Lockscreen ads are the most, shall we say, unpopular Amazon Ads format amongst authors for several reasons. Before we get into those, however, let's first look at what lockscreen ads actually are.

Lockscreen ads appear when a reader turns on their Kindle e-reader or Kindle Fire on the lock screen (original name, I know) and as little banners at the bottom of the screen on these devices, as you can see from the examples below.

Fig. 3.5: An example of a lockscreen ad on a Kindle

When someone clicks on your lockscreen ad, as with sponsored product ads, they are taken directly to your book's product page on Amazon. And you only pay for the click, not the impression.

With lockscreen ads, as they display solely on Kindle devices, you can't advertise paperback or hardback books with them, only e-books.

As I mentioned, there are some issues with lockscreen ads; I've listed them below, in no particular order:

Issue #1: Targeting

One of the primary reasons that lockscreen ads aren't too popular with authors is the targeting, or, more accurately, the *lack* of targeting.

The only targeting you have available to you is a pre-determined list of interests/genres. These interests/genres are incredibly broad and you may struggle to find any relevant options for your book, especially if you write in a niche genre.

Issue #2: Reader Behaviour

As a reader, when I pick up my Kindle, I've got a book in mind that I want to read that's already on my Kindle. With lockscreen ads, as soon as I pick up my Kindle, I'm presented with an ad for a book that I *could* go and buy on Amazon.

But I want to read a book that's on my Kindle already; I'm not in *buying* mode, I'm in *reading* mode.

So, naturally, I swipe away the ad, open the book I want to read that's already on my Kindle, and start reading.

Lockscreen ads can create friction. But maybe that's just me!

Issue #3: Accidental Clicks

You'll often see that lockscreen ads generate lots of clicks, but very few sales. This is because the "call-to-action" button on the ad (i.e., "Read Now") is clicked by readers accidentally.

And remember, with Amazon Ads, you pay for clicks, not impressions.

Issue #4: No Daily Budget Option

The other potential stumbling block with lockscreen ads, particularly if you don't have too much surplus cash to test them with, is that the minimum budget is $100, which, for some authors, can be a complete non-starter.

This budget is spread over a time period that you define, rather than setting a daily budget, so you have a little less control over budgets than you do with the other Amazon Ads formats.

However, there is a way around this ...

Let's say you have $100 that you're happy to lose (potentially) and spend it on testing lockscreen ads.

And let's assume you're only comfortable spending $5 per day. If you set the end date on your lockscreen ad 20 days after your start date, at a maximum of $5 per day, you'll know that you won't spend more than $100 over that 20-day period. Most likely, you'll spend a lot less than $5 per day, but at least you know you won't be spending more than your $100 budget over the next 20 days.

Should You Use Lockscreen Ads?

Despite highlighting all these issues, I'm actually *not* all about lockscreen ads bashing! The one thing they are good at is creating brand (book) awareness. They can position your book in front of huge numbers of your ideal readers on their reading devices; it's just a shame that only a small proportion of these eyeballs result in sales.

Who knows, perhaps, over time, lockscreen ads will vastly improve and I'll be eating my words!

So, whilst lockscreen ads can work, I recommend starting your quest into Amazon Ads with sponsored product ads until you've built up your confidence with the platform as a whole (planning, researching, building, launching, optimizing, scaling, etc.). I'd hold off on lockscreen ads until you can afford to spend $100 or more on testing.

Now you have a better understanding of the three Amazon Ads formats, in the next chapter, we're going to be diving into the topic of bidding: the cornerstone of Amazon Ads.

Chapter Four

Amazon Ads Bidding

With each of the three Amazon Ads formats we covered in the previous chapter (sponsored products, sponsored brands and lockscreen ads), if nobody clicks on your ad, you don't pay a cent, a dime, a penny, to Amazon. This form of advertising is known as pay-per-click (PPC) for obvious reasons. As an advertiser, you bid a certain amount of money that you are prepared to pay for a single click.

Now, we obviously want people to click on your ad so that you can make sales, introduce readers to you, your brand, and your books.

However, even if people aren't clicking on your ad, at the very least, you're positioning your books in front of people, so it's a great way to build discovery and brand awareness – for free.

Throughout this book, I'll be showing you how to ensure that the *right* people are clicking on your Amazon Ads; you don't want just anybody clicking if they aren't your ideal readers, because this will cost you money with little to no chance of them actually buying (and reading) your book.

Bidding on Amazon Ads is a hot topic amongst the author community. There is no right or wrong way to bid; there is only the *right* bid for you.

The amount you bid will depend on several variables, including but not limited to:

- Your core objective
- Your strategy
- How many books are in your series/catalog

- The genre you write in
- Whether your books are in Kindle Unlimited
- Whether you write standalone books or you write in a series
- What you are prepared to pay for a lead/prospect

So, how do you know what your starting bid should be if this is your first foray into Amazon Ads?

When setting up your Amazon Ads, Amazon will provide you with a "suggested bid" and a "bid range," based on the targets you have selected (e.g., keywords, categories, products – topics we'll be diving into on Days 3 and 4 of this book).

You could base your bids on the suggested bid, however, I have found from all the Amazon Ads I have run that the suggested bids aren't overly accurate.

I prefer to work off the bid ranges Amazon provides. And with these numbers, there are two approaches you can choose from:

- Start with high bids (top of the bid range *) and ***decrease*** my bid until I find an equilibrium point of good sales/page reads and a reasonable cost per click.
- Start with low bids (bottom of the bid range) and ***increase*** my bid until I find an equilibrium point of good sales/page reads and a reasonable cost per click.

If a suggested bid range (top or bottom) is more than $1 when starting a new campaign, I don't bid that high! I'll bid up to $0.98 maximum, even if the top of the suggested bid range is $2.38. That is too high a bid to start with, in my opinion, and you can still gather data with a $0.98 bid.

The latter option of starting with a low bid and increasing over time is generally the slowest approach, but also the safest. So, if you're not in a rush (which you never should be with Amazon Ads), are perhaps a little risk averse, or you are only prepared to commit a small budget to Amazon Ads, then this is a great way to begin.

Depending on the genre of the book(s) you're advertising and the targeting option you are using (something we'll cover in much more detail on Days 3 and 4), a low bid could be anywhere from $0.02 to $0.50, or even higher! Not overly useful, I know, but stick with me.

With this slow, steady, and safe approach to bidding, I recommend starting with a bid of between $0.30 and $0.40, even if the low number of the bid range is higher than this. You will soon learn if this bid is too low if you receive no or low impressions (the number of times your ads are shown). Bidding lower than $0.30 is unlikely to garner many impressions, clicks, and sales.

If you have a larger budget to put towards Amazon Ads and are less risk averse, then starting with a higher bid could be for you. You will typically see results much quicker with this approach, sometimes not the results you want to see if you're getting clicks but no sales, but results and data nonetheless.

My preferred approach ... Start with a high bid and lower over time as I start to collect data.

Once again, a high bid for one book could be very different to a high bid for another book and will also depend on the targeting option you are using. Some targets on Amazon Ads could cost you more than $2 for a single click!

If this high-bid approach suits you more than the low-bid approach, bid an amount towards the top end of the bid range of your selected targets. Then, over time, you can reduce your bid by $0.03 – $0.10 cents every five to seven days until you find that sweet spot of strong sales/page reads and a CPC that works for you.

Ultimately, with bidding, only bid what you are prepared to lose, particularly during the testing phase when you are just dipping your toe in the water with Amazon Ads.

Chapter Five

Are You Ready for Amazon Ads?

A s creative people, we authors sometimes see our books as works of art; which they are, of course. With advertising, however, we need to rethink this philosophy and see our books instead as products.

If there's one thing I want you to take away from this chapter, it's this:

Amazon Ads don't sell your book; your book sells your book.

Or, more specifically, your book *product page* sells your book.

On a very basic level, the only role Amazon Ads are playing is driving traffic to your book product page – that's it; providing, of course, that you are sending *relevant* traffic to your book. The various assets on the product page will sell your book.

Ultimately, no amount of advertising is going to sell a poor-quality book (or any product, for that matter).

You may be wondering which assets on your product page I'm talking about. Here they are, in order of importance, based on my experience:

1. Book cover (as this forms part of the ad and drives people to your book)
2. Blurb/book description
3. Reviews (number of reviews and overall rating – forms part of the ad)
4. Look-inside
5. Title and subtitle (this forms part of the ad too)
6. Price (again, this forms part of the ad)

It goes without saying that you also need to write an outstanding book that appeals to your ideal readers, hits the genre tropes if you're writing to market (fiction) or solves a specific problem (if you write non-fiction).

As you can see, there are a few different areas we, as authors, have control over on our product page. Yes, you could send truckloads of traffic to your book product page, but the chances of you generating any sales or page reads are, unfortunately, slim to none if any of the following are true:

- The book cover is poor (you might struggle to generate traffic in the first place if you have an unprofessional book cover);
- The book description doesn't excite and engage the reader or meet their expectations based on the title and subtitle;
- You have little to no reviews (or poor reviews);
- The look-inside of your book shows poor formatting, and the reader doesn't like what they read, sees spelling/grammar mistakes, etc.;
- The title and subtitle don't excite the reader; or
- The price is too high for your genre.

...

Your time will be well spent creating the best product page for your book as you can. This is your sales page; your 24/7 salesperson. It's where potential readers of your book are going to decide whether or not to buy.

As this book is all about Amazon Ads, I'm not going to dive into too much detail about everything to do on your book product page, as otherwise this would be a very long read!

Aside from your book product page, in my experience, there are a few other best practices that can really give you an edge with your Amazon Ads:

- At least 20+ reviews (100+ is better for conversions)
- A best seller rank below 100,000 (below 50,000 would be even better)
- Have a good sales history over the past few months (at least two to three sales and/or borrows per day)

If your books don't meet these best practices, it's not to say that Amazon Ads won't work for you; it's just going to be a little harder, and potentially slightly more expensive, to advertise using Amazon Ads.

Amazon has built an incredible business with a highly customer-centric ethos, meaning that they aim to provide their customers with the best possible experience of shopping with them. This is why customer reviews are such an integral part of Amazon's success.

Also known as "social proof," reviews help potential customers decide if the product they are considering purchasing – in our case, books – is right for them. The more positive reviews there are, the higher the chance of conversion (purchase).

This isn't to say that books with little to no reviews won't succeed with Amazon Ads; but, if you think about it, if you're sending oodles of traffic to your book with Amazon Ads and you have one review/rating, there isn't much in the way of social proof or trust built up there for the customer, particularly if they have never come across your books before.

Compare this with an alternative scenario advertising a book with 157 reviews/ratings, and now the customer feels much more reassured that this is a good book and worth both their time and money.

Keep in mind, also, that the number of reviews/ratings and the overall star rating of your advertised books appear within your Amazon Ads. So, before people even click on your ad, they have an idea of the quality of your book.

Amazon itself recommends having at least 15 reviews/ratings on a book before advertising it with Amazon Ads. Personally, as I mentioned above, I have seen better results with 20+ reviews/ratings. When you reach 100+ reviews/ratings, however, that's when you will start to see a spike in conversions from your Amazon Ads.

My ultimate goal for this chapter was to impress upon you the importance of the role your book product page plays in running successful Amazon Ads, or any form of marketing or advertising, for that matter.

The last thing I want is for you to set up your first Amazon Ads, send reams of traffic to your book product page, but then generate little to no sales because your product page wasn't doing a good job of selling your book.

Now you have a better understanding of the importance your book product page plays in your success with Amazon Ads, let's set up your Amazon Ads account.

Chapter Six

Account Setup

G etting started with Amazon Ads is extremely straightforward. As you're reading this book, I'm assuming that you already have at least one book published on Amazon through your KDP (Kindle Direct Publishing) dashboard.

If not, head on over to kdp.amazon.com, set up your account, and upload your book.

Once you've done that, this chapter (and the rest of this book, in fact) will make a lot more sense!

Book published through KDP? Great, let's move on ...

To get your Amazon Ads account set up, head on over to your KDP dashboard (kdp.amazon.com), go to your *Bookshelf*, and click on the *Promote and Advertise* button next to the book that you want to advertise, as you can see in the image below:

Fig. 6.1

Once you've clicked *Promote and Advertise*, you'll see another screen that looks similar to the screenshot below.

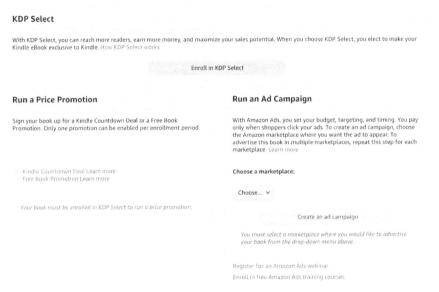

The 7 Day Authors Guide To Amazon Ads

Promote your book on Amazon

KDP Select

With KDP Select, you can reach more readers, earn more money, and maximize your sales potential. When you choose KDP Select, you elect to make your Kindle eBook exclusive to Kindle. How KDP Select works

Enroll in KDP Select

Run a Price Promotion

Sign your book up for a Kindle Countdown Deal or a Free Book Promotion. Only one promotion can be enabled per enrollment period.

Kindle Countdown Deal Learn more
Free Book Promotion Learn more

Your book must be enrolled in KDP Select to run a price promotion.

Run an Ad Campaign

With Amazon Ads, you set your budget, targeting, and timing. You pay only when shoppers click your ads. To create an ad campaign, choose the Amazon marketplace where you want the ad to appear. To advertise this book in multiple marketplaces, repeat this step for each marketplace. Learn more

Choose a marketplace:

Choose... ∨

Create an ad campaign

You must select a marketplace where you would like to advertise your book from the drop-down menu above.

Register for an Amazon Ads webinar
Enroll in free Amazon Ads training courses

Fig. 6.2

Scroll down to the *Run an Ad Campaign* section and choose the marketplace you'd like to advertise in. At the time of writing, the Amazon Marketplaces you can run Amazon Ads in are:

- Amazon.com (USA)
- Amazon.co.uk (UK)
- Amazon.de (Germany)
- Amazon.fr (France)
- Amazon.it (Italy)
- Amazon.es (Spain)
- Amazon.ca (Canada)

- Amazon.com.au (Australia)

Once you've chosen the marketplace you'd like to advertise in, click the yellow *Create an ad campaign* button.

If this is the first time you've run Amazon Ads, you will be required to sign up for an Amazon Advertising account.

Use the same login details you use to login to your KDP account, as this will link your Amazon Advertising account to your KDP account, making things much easier going forward.

IMPORTANT: At the time of writing, you will need a separate Amazon Advertising account for every country you want to advertise in; you will also need to set up separate billing for each account.

As an example, if you wanted to advertise on Amazon.com, Amazon.co.uk, and Amazon.com.au, you would need three separate Amazon Advertising accounts; all would be linked to your KDP Account if you follow the instructions above.

This can be a bit of a nuisance initially, but if you bookmark each of the Amazon Ads dashboards in Google Chrome, Safari (or whichever internet browser you use), you can quickly access each advertising account with the click of a button (assuming that you're already logged in to your KDP account).

Before you run any ads, you'll also need to provide your payment details once you're logged in to your Amazon Advertising account, which you can do via the *Billing and Payments* option in the *Administration* main menu on the left-hand side of your Amazon Ads dashboard.

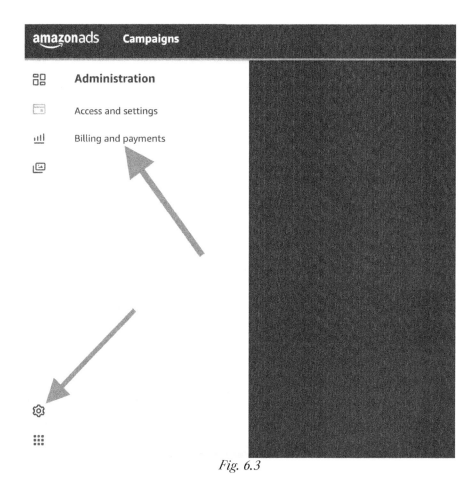

Fig. 6.3

And that's it, your Amazon Ads account is set up and ready to go. I'll be giving you a whistle-stop tour of the Amazon Ads dashboard later on in this book, so don't feel overwhelmed just yet if this is the first time you've seen it; all will become clear ...

Next up, we're moving on to something I call the "Amazon Ads Funnel," which is going to set you apart from other advertisers.

Before we do that, however, your first Action Step ...

Action Step for Day 1

Set Up Your Amazon Ads Account

This first Action Step is quick and easy! Just follow the instructions in the last chapter of Day 1 to set up your Amazon Ads account and your billing information, so that when we arrive at Day 3, you're ready to build and launch your first Amazon Ads.

Download the Amazon Ads Toolkit

To help you implement everything I'm about to share with you in this book, I highly recommend saving yourself hours of time by downloading my FREE Amazon Ads Toolkit.

www.matthewjholmes.com/acos

It has many beneficial and valuable tools, including the Amazon Ads targeting tool, which is a spreadsheet I have built from the ground up that I use every single day when managing Amazon Ads for authors.

Inside the targeting tool, you will be able to collect all the relevant data for your campaigns that we'll be setting up together throughout this book and keep track of what works and what doesn't.

Day 2

The Amazon Ads Funnel

B elieve it or not, there is a process for running profitable and effective Amazon Ads. Just throwing a bunch of keywords at Amazon isn't a strategy; it's hope marketing, and it will not serve you well.

In Day 2, I'm going to walk you through the three-step Amazon Ads funnel I use in every Amazon Ads account I manage to create a systematic, easy-to-follow process, ensuring you are spending your hard-earned money in the most efficient and profitable way.

Chapter Seven

Focusing on the 80/20

I n 1948, Vilfredo Federico Damaso Pareto was born in Italy. Years later, after becoming a philosopher and economist, keen gardener Pareto was tending to his homegrown peas when he noticed that 20% of the pea plants were generating 80% of the healthy pea pods.

It got Pareto thinking about the topic of uneven distribution, and not just in his garden. Looking at wealth in his homeland to begin with, he discovered that 80% of the land in Italy was owned by just 20% of the population.

He next switched his focus to a variety of different industries and found the same ratio applied yet again: around 80% of production typically came from just 20% of the companies within each industry.

He made more and more discoveries just like this in all walks of life, so Pareto's generalization became:

80% of results will come from 20% of the action.

This, in turn, became known as "the 80/20 rule" or "Pareto's Principle." And this imbalance can be seen everywhere; even in your own wardrobe, where you'll typically wear 20% of your clothes, 80% of the time.

Whilst not an exact science, the 80/20 ratio of Pareto's Principle is also very present within your Amazon Ads:

Around 20% of your keywords will generate 80% of your sales. Knowing this, we can use the 80/20 rule to our advantage by doubling down on what is *actually* working with our Amazon Ads because, as I'm sure you

have figured out by now, the majority of your Amazon Ads targeting won't work (around 80% to be exact!).

The Amazon Ads funnel I use when managing Amazon Ads for authors uses this very philosophy.

So, without further ado, now you have an understanding of what the 80/20 rule is, let's apply it to your Amazon Ads.

Chapter Eight

The Three Phases of the Amazon Ads Funnel

As the title of this chapter describes, there are three phases of the Amazon Ads funnel:

- **DISCOVERY**
- **RESEARCH**
- **PERFORMANCE**

Before we dive into each one, there's one more piece of crucial information for you to understand: Amazon Ads campaign structure.

As you can see in the diagram below, there are three levels to the Amazon Ads campaign structure:

- Campaign
- Ad Group
- Ad

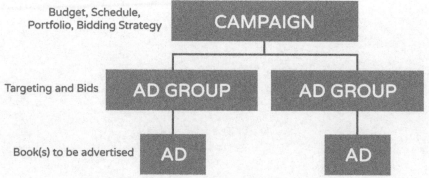

Fig. 8.1: The Amazon Ads campaign structure

The **Campaign** level is where you will set the budget and bidding strategy (i.e., how much you want to spend per day and how aggressive you want to be with your overall bidding strategy).

The **Ad Group** level is where you tell Amazon which keywords, ASINs, or categories you want to target within this campaign.

And the **Ad** level is the creative that readers see when they are browsing Amazon, looking for their next book to read.

You can have multiple campaigns within your Amazon Ads account (thousands of campaigns if you need them!), and each campaign works independently of the other campaigns within your account.

So, that's a brief overview of the Amazon Ads campaigns structure; now let's jump back into the Amazon Ads funnel, which will make far more sense now that you understand campaign structure.

The best way for me to describe the Amazon Ads funnel in action is to show you a visual representation:

Fig. 8.2: The Amazon Ads funnel

As you can see, the discovery and research campaigns feed into the performance campaigns. I also separate out the different types of targeting to keywords and ASINs, because they perform very differently and have different purposes.

I'll be dedicating the next three days of this book (Days 3, 4, and 5) to each of these three phases, but to wrap up this chapter, I'd like to give you a small taste of each phase to help solidify your understanding of the role they play in the Amazon Ads funnel.

Discovery Phase

The discovery phase is where we are leaning on Amazon to do a lot of the research for us, using two of the quickest types of campaigns you can set up with Amazon Ads:

- Automatic targeting campaign
- Category targeting campaign

Both campaigns are casting a wide net, giving Amazon relatively free rein on what it does with our money. This may sound a little scary, but trust me, these campaigns can work like gangbusters!

Automatic targeting and category targeting campaigns are relatively hands off: they take just a minute or two to set up and can run for many months, if not years, with very little input from you, aside from a little optimization, which we'll be covering on day 6. They can also be scaled up easily, providing they have been well optimized.

Research Phase

The research phase is where you have a lot more control over what you are targeting. Personally, I target the following:

- Author names
- Genre search terms (e.g., crime thriller, gardening for beginners, historical fantasy novels, etc.)
- ASINs (every book on Amazon has a unique code known as an ASIN; with Amazon Ads, you can be highly granular and target specific ASINs)

One highly important note to make here regards *relevance*.

As I've covered previously, Amazon aims to provide its customers with the best possible shopping experience; it does this by showing only the most relevant products (in our case, books) based on customer behaviour, such as what they are searching for or what books they are looking at.

It does this to, yes, provide a great experience for customers, but also because Amazon knows if they show a customer a relevant book, they are more likely to buy, so Amazon are happy as well as the customer and the author.

So, with your Amazon Ads, ensure that you always have *relevance* in mind when deciding what keywords, categories, and ASINs to target. This will not only help your sales but also help to keep your costs as low as possible because Amazon rewards relevance.

In the research phase, I keep each targeting type in a separate campaign because it helps immensely with account management, as I can clearly see from the campaign name what is being targeted within that campaign, as well as what type of targeting is working. So, I have at least three campaigns in the research phase:

- 1 x campaign targeting authors
- 1 x campaign targeting genre search terms
- 1 x campaign targeting ASINs

I will cover the nuances of each of these campaigns in their associated chapters over the coming days.

Performance Phase

The third and final phase relates to performance. This is where the rubber meets the road and where the 80/20 rule really comes into play.

As we saw from the Amazon Ads funnel diagram earlier in this chapter, keywords and ASINs from the discovery and research phases feed directly into the performance phase campaigns.

My threshold for when a keyword or ASIN is graduated into the relevant performance campaign is when they have generated at least two or more sales/borrows in the discovery or research campaign they originated from.

When they have been graduated into the performance phase, I see them as proven, so I am much more aggressive with them here, bidding higher and putting more budget behind them.

I have at least two performance campaigns in any one account:

- 1 x campaign for proven keywords
- 1 x campaign for proven ASINs

I will dive much deeper into the performance phase on Day 5 and will show you how I set these campaigns up.

For now though, that's going to wrap up this chapter on the Amazon Ads funnel.

Next up, on Day 3, we're going to be setting up the two campaigns that will form the discovery phase of your Amazon Ads funnel.

Action Step for Day 2

Create Your Amazon Ads Funnel Portfolios

C reate four portfolios in your Amazon Ads account by following the steps below.

Think of portfolios as folders within your Amazon Ads account. You can have multiple portfolios in your account and choose to add certain campaigns into certain portfolios to help keep everything organized.

I like to have one portfolio for each stage of the Amazon Ads funnel for every series or book I'm advertising, as well as an additional portfolio for brand campaigns, using the series title rather than the book title in the portfolio name (I'll be covering brand campaigns on Day 7, but setting up your brand portfolio now will ensure you're ready to roll on Day 7).

For example, with my wife's books, as her series is best enjoyed when read in order, we focus the majority of the budget on the first title, *The Forbidden*. So, the portfolio structure I use looks like this:

- 1 | The Forbidden [DISCOVERY]
- 2 | The Forbidden [RESEARCH]
- 3 | The Forbidden [PERFORMANCE]
- 4 | The Ancestors Saga [BRAND]

Another benefit of portfolios is that you can set up "budget caps" that recur monthly, or can run between a particular start and end date.

When all the campaigns within that portfolio have a combined total ad spend that reaches your set budget cap, the campaigns will stop delivering until you either remove or increase the budget cap, the end date of your budget cap is reached, or a new month rolls around.

Budget caps are a great way to ensure you don't exceed your Amazon Ads monthly budget allocation.

To create your portfolios:

1. Head on over to your Amazon Ads dashboard and click the + *Create a portfolio* button, highlighted below:

Fig. 8.3

2. Name your portfolio accordingly, and then click the *Create a portfolio* button

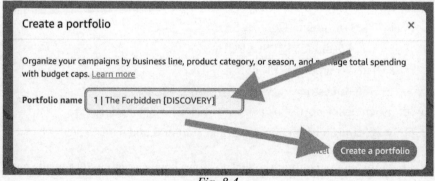

Fig. 8.4

3. Repeat the steps above for each portfolio you need to create (one for discovery, one for research, one for performance and one for brand)

Day 3

The Discovery Phase

T his is where it all begins ... The discovery phase is the first stage of the Amazon Ads funnel, consisting of two very simple, very quick campaigns that we are going to set up together.

So, without further ado, let's get into it ...

Chapter Nine

Automatic Targeting Campaign Overview

As the name suggests, an automatic targeting campaign does 95% of the heavy lifting for you! This targeting option allows Amazon to venture out and test different keywords and ASINs that *it* believes are relevant to your advertised book(s).

Your only input is deciding on your maximum daily budget and determining how much you are prepared to pay for a single click on your ad. You also have control over what not to target through the use of negative targeting, but that is something we'll cover on Day 6, Optimization for Growth.

What you *cannot* do with automatic targeting campaigns is choose specific keyword and ASINs to target; this is something we will be doing through the use of manual targeting on Day 4 (tomorrow).

Automatic targeting campaigns rely on Amazon's knowledge of your book; it will be choosing keywords and ASINs to target on your behalf, based on various assets of your book, such as:

- Title
- Subtitle
- Keywords
- Categories your book is listed in

There's also debate over whether automatic targeting uses your book description; personally, I'm on the side of the fence that believes automatic targeting *does* trawl your book description, but I could be wrong.

The algorithm is also going to take past performance of your book into account; more specifically, which other books people have bought before or after they bought your book.

Once the data has started to roll into your Amazon Ads dashboard, you can actually see which ASINs and keywords have triggered your ad to show and which of these have generated sales and/or page reads if your books are in Kindle Unlimited.

If there are keywords or ASINs that are irrelevant to your book or have not generated sales after a certain number of clicks, you can add these to the negative targeting options in your campaign, which will prevent the automatic targeting campaign from showing your ads on these targets in the future. As I say, though, this is a topic for Day 6.

So, before you set up an automatic targeting campaign, take some time to review your KDP keywords and categories to make sure they are still relevant to your book. If they're not relevant, carry out some keyword research and change them; irrelevant keywords and categories can severely impact the results you achieve with automatic targeting.

Automatic targeting is a hotly contested topic amongst authors; some people love them, some people never touch them.

To help you decide whether automatic targeting is right for you, here are some pros and cons based on my experience. As with everything else in this book, however, I encourage you to test them and see how they perform for *your* books, before deciding whether or not they are a good fit for you.

Pros of Automatic Targeting

- Quick to set up (you can have a campaign up and running within a minute or two)
- Can produce great results (though can be a bit hit and miss, depending on genre)

- Find keywords and ASIN targets you may never have thought of that you can scale up

Cons of Automatic Targeting

- Leaving the fate of your campaign in the hands of the Amazon algorithm
- They can spiral out of control (but easy to turn them off or reduce spend)
- Lack of control by only being able to impact bids, budget, and negative targeting

Yes, there are a few cons to automatic targeting campaigns, but I believe they are far outweighed by the pros and automatic targeting can be an absolute game-changer for your Amazon Ads.

So, I highly recommend you use automatic targeting campaigns in the discovery phase of your Amazon Ads funnel; and, in the next chapter, I'll be walking you through step-by-step how to launch your first one.

Chapter Ten

Launching Your Automatic Targeting Campaign

Y our account is set up. Your book product page is optimized for conversion. Now it's time to put this plan into action by launching your first campaign in the discovery phase of your Amazon Ads funnel ...

The Automatic Targeting Campaign

Without further ado, let's dive right into the step-by-step of launching your automatic targeting campaign; this is the exact process I follow when launching these campaigns for my author clients, so follow closely and watch the sales roll in.

Step 1

Head on over to your Amazon Ads account by going to **www.advertising .amazon.com**. If you haven't already done so, I highly recommend that you bookmark your Amazon Ads dashboard for quick access moving forward.

Step 2

Once you're in your Amazon Ads dashboard, you may feel slightly overwhelmed at what you see, but don't panic, we'll be delving into every aspect of the dashboard on Day 6, when we start looking at the data and optimizing your ads.

For now, though, to start your first Amazon Ads campaign, all you need to do is simply click on the *Create campaign* button, as highlighted below.

Fig. 10.1

If you're advertising on Amazon.com, you'll now see a screen similar to the screenshot below, where you have the option to choose from the three different Amazon Ads formats we discussed on Day 1:

- *Sponsored Products*
- *Sponsored Brands*
- *Lockscreen Ads*

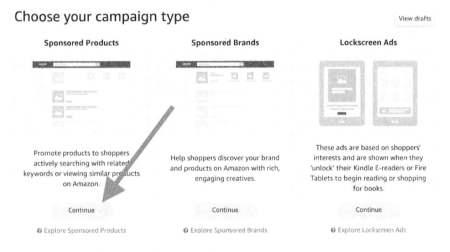

Fig. 10.2

If you're advertising outside of Amazon.com (e.g., Amazon.co.uk), at the time of writing, you will only see the *Sponsored Products* and *Sponsored Brands* options. In some marketplaces, you will only see *Sponsored Products* available.

Wherever you're advertising, however, you will be able to create the ad we're going to build together in this chapter.

So, click the *Continue* button underneath the *Sponsored Products* option.

Step 3

The next screen you'll see will be the campaign creation page, and, if you're advertising on Amazon.com, the first thing to do here is choose your *Ad Format*, of which there are two options:

- *Custom text ad*
- *Standard ad*

Fig. 10.3

*IMPORTANT: If you are advertising on Amazon.co.uk or any marketplace outside of Amazon.com, you won't have the option to choose an **Ad Format**. By default, in all marketplaces outside of Amazon.com, **Standard ad** will be used.*

*At the time of writing, Amazon.com has a slightly different campaign set-up process to some other marketplaces, but the details you are required to enter remain the same in each marketplace, aside from the **Ad Format** option we've just been through.*

Custom text ad allows you to write a short blurb for your book that may or may not appear next to your ad. It's down to Amazon's discretion whether they choose to show the *Custom text* on your ad.

Standard ad doesn't give you the option to write any ad text.

Custom text is there to entice the reader to click on your ad. Bear in mind that you're limited to 150 characters (including spaces) for your *Custom text ad*, so you have very little space to compel a reader to click.

Personally, from all the testing I have done, I haven't seen any noticeable difference in performance with ads that use the *Custom text ad* format and ads that use the *Standard ad* format.

With a *Standard ad,* you can advertise multiple books in a single campaign, whereas with a *custom text ad,* you can only advertise one book.

Another feature of using the *Standard ad* format is that you can have multiple ad groups within a single campaign, which can be helpful in certain scenarios. For now, though, we'll keep things simple and stick to one ad group per campaign.

Step 4

I recommend you choose *Standard ad* (which won't allow you to add custom text), and you will now see a new box where you can add an *Ad group name.* As a reminder from Day 2, an ad group is simply a folder within a campaign; within each ad group, you define the book you are advertising, the targeting (e.g., keywords) and the bids.

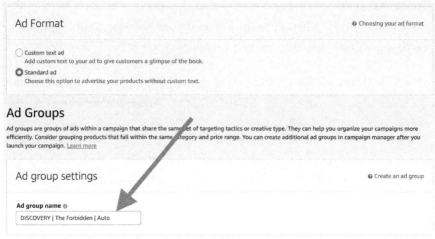

Fig. 10.4

When you only have a few campaigns in your Amazon Ads account, it's easy to gloss over developing a consistent, clear, understandable naming convention to use on all your campaigns and ad groups. But when you have 10, 20, 30, or more campaigns, a clear naming convention that you use with every single one is going to be an enormous help in seeing the details of a particular campaign at a glance and making the management of your account that much more efficient.

I highly recommend that you start as you mean to go on and create a naming convention system that works for you.

To keep my naming conventions simple and understandable, I keep the *Ad group name* and the campaign name exactly the same. Here's how I name my ad groups and campaigns, but feel free to develop a naming convention that works for you:

[FUNNEL PHASE] | [BOOK TITLE] | [CAMPAIGN TYPE/TARGETING]

To put this into some context for you, here is the name of a campaign in my wife's Amazon Ads account for the automatic targeting campaign:

DISCOVERY | The Forbidden | Auto

So, name your ad group how you wish, and let's move on.

Step 5

All you need to do here is click the *Add* button next to the book you want to advertise from the list on the left-hand side. Your chosen book will then appear in the right-hand column.

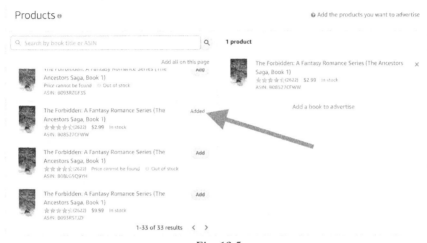

Fig. 10.5

If you are using the *Standard ad* format, as I do, you will be able to add multiple books into the same ad group. If, instead, you are using the *Custom text ad* format, you will only be able to add one book into a single campaign.

Step 6

The next step is very simple; choosing between *Automatic targeting* and *Manual targeting*.

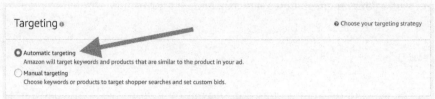

Fig. 10.6

Automatic targeting is chosen by default, so as we are setting up an automatic targeting campaign, there's nothing to do here!

Step 7

Up next is bidding. The default option is *Set default bid*. For best results with automatic targeting, I don't recommend you use this option. Instead, choose the *Set bids by targeting group* option.

Fig. 10.7

The four *Automatic Targeting* groups are:

- *Close match:* Targets search terms that are closely related to your advertised book
- *Loose match:* Targets search terms that are loosely related to your advertised book
- *Substitutes:* Targets ASINs (i.e., other books) that are similar to your advertised book
- *Complements:* Targets ASINs (i.e., other books) that are loosely related to your advertised book

As you can see from the screenshot above, Amazon provides us with some *Suggested Bids* which are based on the book you're advertising in this ad group, as well as what other advertisers in similar genres are paying for clicks on their ads.

It is possible to turn off particular targeting groups; however, to begin with, I recommend keeping all the targeting groups turned on; you can turn off poor performing targeting groups once this campaign has been running for a few weeks or months and you have gathered enough statistically significant data to make those sorts of decisions.

I generally recommend bidding slightly higher on the *Close match* and *Loose match* targeting groups, with *Close match* being the highest bid of all. I also suggest bidding a few cents lower on *Substitutes* and *Complements*, with *Complements* being the lowest bid.

My reasoning for this, in most cases, is because *Complements* will usually generate a lot of clicks, but you may not see a great conversion rate (i.e., clicks turning into sales and/or page reads). Whereas search terms (*Close match* and *Loose match*), tend to generate fewer clicks but have a higher conversion rate.

I have also found that *Substitutes* generally receives the least amount of budget, and therefore clicks, and is the worst performer. If your books are enrolled in Kindle Unlimited, you may find, as I have, that the *Complements* and *Loose match* targeting groups generate the most page reads (called "KENP read" by Amazon).

As I mentioned on Day 1, there are a couple of different ways you can bid on Amazon Ads:

- Start with low bids and gradually increase
- Start with high bids and gradually decrease

So, choose how you'd like to bid (low or high).

Let's say that I'm working with a small budget and need to be conservative with my bids. If the suggested bid range for the *Close match* targeting group was $0.55 - $1.38, I would bid around $0.58 for *Close match*. I would then bid $0.01-$0.02 lower for each of the other targeting groups; so, my bids would look like this:

Close match: $0.58

Loose match: $0.57

Substitutes: $0.56

Complements: $0.54

If your bids for other targeting groups aren't above the bottom of the suggested bid range, don't worry, you may still receive impressions, clicks, and sales. The suggested bid range is purely there as a guide.

If, after seven days, your campaign as a whole or a particular targeting group isn't generating many/any clicks or impressions, I would recommend increasing the bids on the relevant targeting group(s) by 10% to see if that new bid is enough for the algorithm to start taking notice of you.

Step 8

Once you have set your bids for each targeting group, if you continue scrolling down the page, you will see two additional sections:

- *Negative keyword targeting*

- *Negative product targeting*

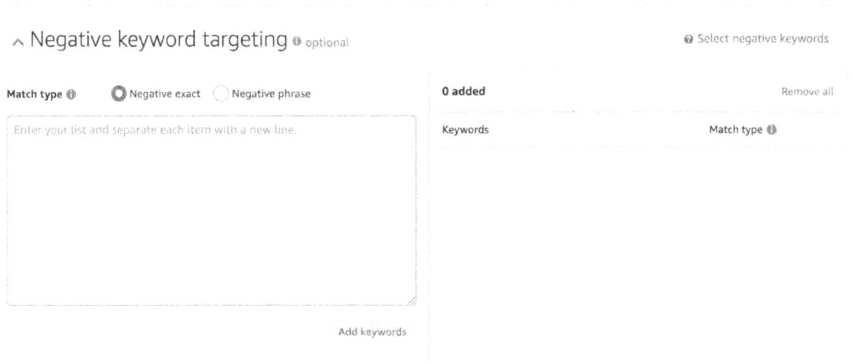

Fig. 10.8

Negative targeting allows you to define particular words or ASINs (books) that you do not want your campaign to be associated with.

For your first campaign, if your book is paid (i.e., not available for free), I recommend adding the word "free" to the *Negative keyword targeting* list as a *Negative phrase match*. This will prevent your ad from showing whenever somebody types a search term that includes the word "free" in it, such as "free fantasy books."

If your book *is* available for free, don't add "free" as a negative keyword!

At this stage, I wouldn't recommend adding any other negative keywords or targets, unless you already have enough statistically significant data to negate a particular keyword.

Let Amazon do its thing; don't throttle it by stacking up too many restrictions. You can always come back later and add negative keywords and targets if needs be, once you have collected some data.

We'll be diving much deeper into negative targeting on Day 6 when we start optimizing campaigns, as you can negate keywords and ASINs at any time during the life of a campaign or ad group.

Step 9

The final step of launching your automatic targeting campaign is the campaign settings, of which there are two sections. The first is your *Campaign bidding strategy*. This is where you decide *how* you want to bid on the keywords you are targeting. Another way of looking at it is how aggressive you want to be with your bidding.

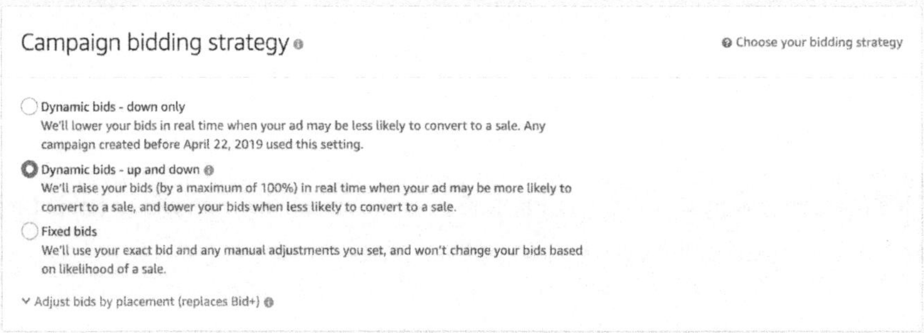

Campaign bidding strategy ⊙   ⊘ Choose your bidding strategy

○ Dynamic bids - down only
We'll lower your bids in real time when your ad may be less likely to convert to a sale. Any
campaign created before April 22, 2019 used this setting.

◉ Dynamic bids - up and down ⊙
We'll raise your bids (by a maximum of 100%) in real time when your ad may be more likely to
convert to a sale, and lower your bids when less likely to convert to a sale.

○ Fixed bids
We'll use your exact bid and any manual adjustments you set, and won't change your bids based
on likelihood of a sale.

⌄ Adjust bids by placement (replaces Bid+) ⊙

Fig. 10.9

There are three bidding strategies to choose from, each with their own pros and cons:

- *Dynamic bids – down only:* Amazon will lower your bids in real-time if its algorithm thinks a click is less likely to convert into a sale of your advertised book.
- *Dynamic bids – up and down:* Amazon will raise your bids by up to 100% if it thinks a click is more likely to convert into a sale, or lower your bid if it thinks a click is less likely to result in a sale.
- *Fixed bids:* Amazon won't make any changes to your bids; they will use your exact bid.

Here are my thoughts on each of the bidding strategies:

- *Dynamic bids – down only* is certainly the safest bidding strategy to use as it provides somewhat of a safety net for you.

- *Dynamic bids – up and down* is something to use when you have a campaign that is working well using the *Dynamic bids – down only* option.
- *Fixed bids* can be a great option to use with new campaigns if you are struggling to get traction with *Dynamic bids - down only*.

The default bidding strategy for automatic targeting campaigns is currently *Dynamic bids – up and down*. Whilst this can be a great bidding strategy for a mature automatic targeting campaign, I have found it be too aggressive for a brand-new campaign.

For now, the safest option I recommend you start with is *Dynamic bids – down only*.

If you have the budget and want to collect data faster, then you can use *Fixed bids* from the start of a new campaign. Keep in mind that, with *Fixed bids*, Amazon will spend your budget quicker than if you use *Dynamic bids – down only*.

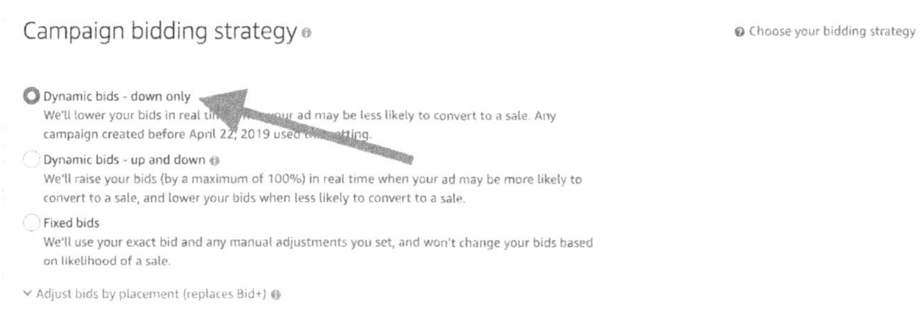

Fig. 10.10

In some cases, if a book I am advertising doesn't have much sales history (i.e., it is ranked poorly and hasn't sold many copies over the past month or two), I would start this automatic targeting campaign using the *Fixed bids* bidding strategy from the beginning.

TOP TIP: *If your Campaign has been running for seven days and you still don't have many/any impressions or clicks, then I would suggest*

changing your bidding strategy to Fixed bids, *as you are forcing Amazon to take your full bid into account, rather than letting them decide when a click is more or less likely to convert into a sale for you.*

Step 10

On the final section of your setup, you need to give your campaign a name. As I covered earlier in this chapter, I use the same name for the ad group as I do for the campaign. So, in this scenario, our campaign name will also be:

DISCOVERY | The Forbidden | Auto

Fig. 10.11

Step 11

Next up, you need to add your automatic targeting campaign into the discovery portfolio you created yesterday, as per the screenshot below.

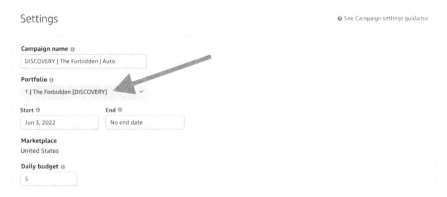

Fig. 10.12

Step 12

Setting a *Start* and *End* date for your campaign is next on the list. I recommend starting your campaign today, which is the default setting, anyway. If you wanted to launch this campaign at some point in the future, you can do that too.

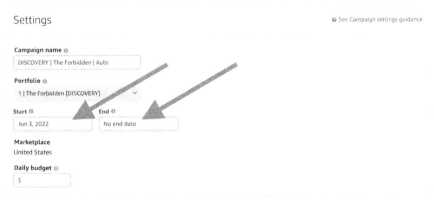

Fig. 10.13

Typically, I prefer to *not* have an end date, unless there's a specific reason, such as a big promotion or launch. I check all the Amazon Ads accounts I manage on a daily basis, so I will manually stop a campaign running if I feel the need to.

If, however, you're worried about forgetting you have campaigns running, you can choose to enter an end date. I would just recommend that you let it run for at least 14 days at a bare minimum, ideally 30 days if you can, as you really need this sort of timeframe to assess whether an Amazon Ads campaign is working for you.

Step 13

The final decision to make on the campaign setup is your *Daily budget*. I recommend you start with at least $10 per day if you can. This is an ideal amount for testing and collecting enough statistically significant data from which to make decisions.

Once you have some solid data and you can see what's working, then you can gradually begin to increase your daily budget.

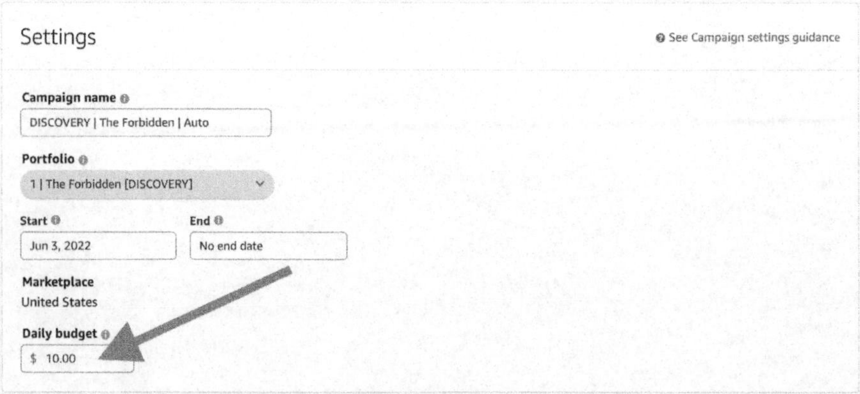

Fig. 10.14

A little quirk of Amazon Ads is that they will not necessarily spend your entire daily budget each day. I have some campaigns with a daily budget of $250 and I'm lucky if they spend $50 of that!

From my experience and testing, I have found that showing Amazon you are prepared to spend a good amount of money each day will make them more inclined to show your ads, generating more impressions, clicks, sales, and, importantly, data.

Step 14

Before you hit the *Launch campaign* button, go right back to the top of the page and double (even triple) check everything. It's easy to miss something as simple as picking the wrong book to advertise or entering the wrong bid amount.

If you've written any *Custom text ad*, read this out loud to yourself – it's amazing the mistakes you pick up!

Once you're happy that everything is correct, go ahead and click *Launch campaign*.

Amazon say that your campaign can take up to 72 hours to be approved and launched. Typically, however, I find my campaigns are live within 12-24 hours; I've even had them live within six hours of setting them up!

Once your campaign has been approved, you'll receive an email from Amazon letting you know it has been "moderated."

This is a strange choice of words, but what you're looking for in the email is that your campaigns is now "eligible." This means that it is now online and will start delivering over the following hours and days. It just takes some time for your campaigns to start generating impressions as Amazon learns the best placements across its ecosystem.

Phew! What a monster of a chapter that was!

So, now you've got your automatic targeting campaign up and running. Let's move on to setting up another campaign, but this time, we're going to give Amazon a little more guidance on where to show your ads through the use of category targeting.

Chapter Eleven

Category Targeting Campaigns Overview

C ategory targeting casts a wide net, similar to automatic targeting, but is a little more refined.

Predominantly, category targeting shows your ads on the product pages of other books, although they can also show your ads on search result pages for keywords related to the books within a particular category, such as:

- Historical thrillers
- Police procedurals
- Self-help time management

This gives you a little more control compared to automatic targeting Campaigns, because you are choosing to target books within specific categories.

You cannot tell Amazon to target specific books within a specific category, but as with automatic targeting campaigns, you can use negative targeting to prevent Amazon from showing your ads on certain book product pages.

Due to this "spaghetti on the wall" targeting, you'll typically see lots of impressions but potentially fewer clicks; though this is by no means a hard and fast rule – some of my best performing Amazon Ads use category targeting.

Category targeting allows you to reach a huge number of readers relatively inexpensively. You will also discover books you didn't know existed that perform well as targets for your books – these are the books you should be scaling up. But I'm getting ahead of myself! We'll be covering scaling on Day 5.

Let's set up your first category targeting campaign!

Chapter Twelve

Launching Your Category Targeting Campaign

L et's jump right into things and launch your first category targeting campaign ...

Step 1

As we did with the automatic targeting campaign, in your Amazon Ads dashboard, click the *Create campaign* button, as highlighted below.

Fig. 12.1

Step 2

Then choose the *Sponsored Products* option when selecting a campaign type.

Fig. 12.2

Step 3

When running category targeting campaigns, I always use multiple ad groups, targeting one category per ad group. To do this, we need to use the *Standard ad* option, so we'll select that first.

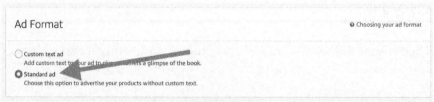

Fig. 12.3

To keep things as organized as possible, I include the category I'm targeting within the ad group name. However, as we don't know what category we're going to be targeting yet, we'll leave the ad group name field blank for the time being and will come back to it shortly.

Step 4

Choose the book(s) you'd like to advertise in this campaign, just as you did with the automatic targeting campaign.

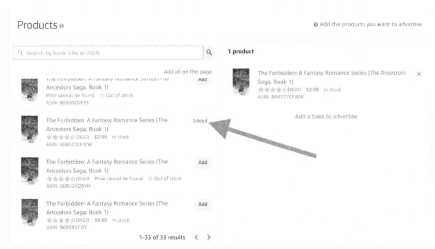

Fig. 12.4

Step 5

We now need to choose between *Automatic targeting* and *Manual targeting*. As we are going to be directing Amazon a little more with our targeting, choose *Manual targeting* here. On the new box that pops up below the *Manual Targeting* heading, choose *Product targeting*.

Your selected options should now look like the screenshot below.

Fig. 12.5

Step 6

Now comes the fun part – choosing the categories!

However, as I mentioned earlier in this chapter, we are going to target just one category per ad group. This prevents the budget being spread across too many targets and helps to improve deliverability of your ads.

In the *Product targeting* section, you will see some new options, where you can choose between *Categories* and *Individual products*.

Product targeting ⓘ
❓ See product targeting guidelines

Categories ⓘ	Individual products ⓘ		0 added			Remove all
Suggested ⓘ Search			Categories & products	Sugg. bid ⓘ *Apply All*	Bid	

Bid	Suggested bid ∨					
9 suggestions		Sugg. bid ⓘ	Add all			
/Kindle Store/Kindle eBooks/Science Fiction & Fantasy/Fantasy/Historical Fantasy **Category:** Historical Fantasy Products: 4,347-7,245		$0.57 $0.28 - $1.01	Add Refine			
/Kindle Store/Kindle eBooks/Science Fiction & Fantasy/Science Fiction/Alternative History **Category:** Alternative History Products: 2,294-3,823		$0.51 $0.32 - $0.85	Add Refine			
/Kindle Store/Kindle eBooks/Science Fiction & Fantasy/Metaphysical Fantasy ... **Category:** Metaphysical Fantasy eBooks Products: 3,195-5,325		$1.05 $0.54 - $1.39	Add Refine			

Fig. 12.6

Categories is selected by default, which is perfect for us at this stage. You may also see that Amazon suggests categories you could target, which are generally fairly accurate.

The other option you have with categories is to search for a specific category you'd like to target within this ad group.

I first review the *Suggested* categories to see if Amazon is recommending anything suitable; as I say, the majority of the time, these categories are highly relevant to the book I am advertising.

If there's a particular category I'd like to target that isn't listed here, I'll instead use the *Search* option and find it that way.

So, choose your category from the list of suggestions, or search for a specific category you'd like to target, by clicking the *Add* button next to your chosen category. Once you have added your category, it will appear on the right-hand side of your screen, as you can see below.

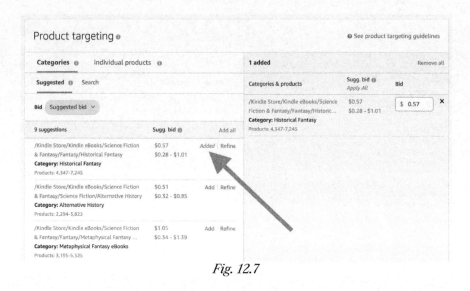

Fig. 12.7

Always remember the core principle of Amazon Ads: relevance. Only choose categories that are relevant to your advertised book.

By all means choose categories that aren't 100% in line with your books, but there should be some resemblance.

What you shouldn't be doing is targeting the romance category if your book is a crime thriller with no hint of a love story.

Doing this will only damage your results and potentially lead to poor reviews if the wrong readers pick up your book through the ads.

You may also experience deliverability issues with your ads because Amazon deems your advertised book irrelevant to your chosen category and, therefore, does not serve them; or, if they do serve them, your impressions (number of times your ads are seen) will be severely throttled.

When selecting categories, it's important to note that there are three types to choose from:

- **Kindle Store:** for example, */Kindle Store/Kindle eBooks/Science Fiction & Fantasy/Science Fiction/Alternative History*
- **Books:** for example, */Books/Literature & Fiction/Genre Literature & Fiction/Metaphysical & Visionary Fiction*
- **Audible Books:** for example, */Audible Books & Originals/Science Fiction & Fantasy*

If you're advertising the Kindle version of your book, make sure you select categories that include *Kindle Store* in their category string. If you're advertising the print version of your book, choose an option which includes *Books* in the category string.

You can't advertise audiobooks with Amazon Ads at the time of writing, so make sure you don't select any categories that include *Audible* in their category string.

Step 7

Next, we need to set a bid for targeting books in this category. The higher your bid, the more readers you are likely to reach.

However, with so many potential targets within a category targeting campaign, your budget can rapidly get eaten up. I therefore recommend that you start your bids relatively low and increase them if you aren't generating many or any impressions after five to seven days.

In the example category targeting campaign I'm setting up here, the *Suggested bid* range is $0.28 – $1.01.

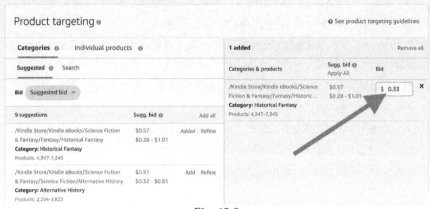

Fig. 12.8

With these numbers, I would use a starting bid of $0.33. Not too high that the budget is going to be spent within a matter of hours, but high enough that we are over the minimum suggested bid of $0.28.

If, after five to seven days, I'm getting very few impressions, then I'll look to generate more by increasing the bid by 10%.

Step 8

You can ignore the negative targeting section of the campaign setup; we won't be negating any ASINs until the campaign has been running for a few days/weeks and we have some data to work with.

So, we'll move on to the *Campaign bidding strategy*.

As with the automatic targeting campaign, I recommend giving yourself a bit of a safety net by starting with *Dynamic bids – down only*.

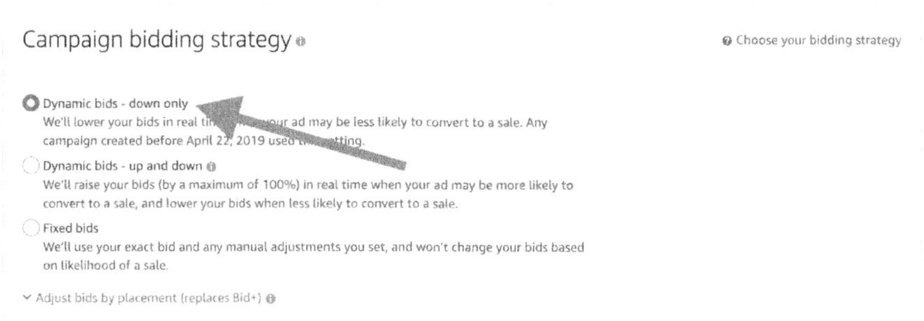

Fig. 12.9

Once you've chosen your bidding strategy, you can move on to the *Settings*.

Step 9

It's time now to name your campaign. Here's how I name my category targeting campaigns:

[PHASE] | [BOOK TITLE] | Categories

In practice, here's how this would look:

DISCOVERY | The Forbidden | Categories

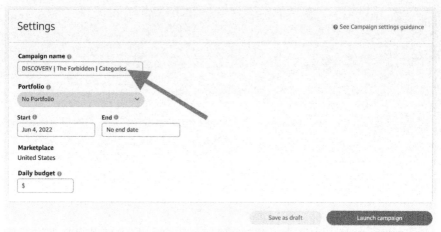

Fig. 12.10

Step 10

I also add category targeting campaigns to the discovery portfolio, so I highly recommend doing this with your campaign too.

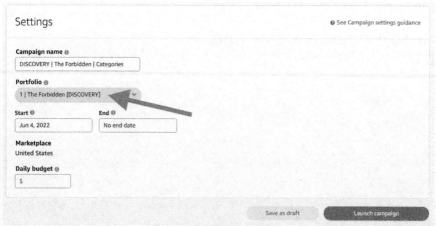

Fig. 12.11

You can leave the *Start* and *End* date as default, unless you have a specific reason you want to start and end your campaigns on certain dates.

Step 11

It's now time to define the daily budget for your category targeting campaign. I recommend keeping your daily budgets relatively low as otherwise your money will quickly disappear!

Typically, I use a $10 per day budget for category targeting campaigns. Once the campaign has been refined over time and is performing well, I will increase the budget slightly to reach more readers.

Keep in mind, though, that with more budget comes more impressions, more clicks, and, very likely, more clicks on irrelevant book product pages or product pages of books that just don't perform well for you. So, when you increase budgets on category targeting campaigns, keep an eye on where the spend is going; this is something I'll be covering with you on Day 6.

For now, though, set a daily budget of at least $10. If you're feeling a little put off by how much category targeting campaigns can spend and how quickly they can spend it, set a daily budget of $5, but no less because you are unlikely to generate much in the way of impressions and clicks, and therefore data, with a budget that low.

Step 12

The final step in setting up your category targeting campaign is to name your ad group. So, scroll back to the top of the page to the *Ad group name* box.

With category targeting campaigns, as I mentioned earlier, I use the category I'm targeting within this ad group in the *Ad group name*:

CAT: [CATEGORY NAME]

In practice, here's what this would look like:

CAT: Historical Fantasy

Fig. 12.12

Step 13

Finally, review all the settings on this page and, once you're happy with everything, click the *Launch campaign* button!

Step 14

Now we need to target some additional categories within this same campaign and reach even more readers. Targeting multiple categories also allows us to test which categories are going to perform best for our books.

To do this, find the category targeting campaign you've just launched in your Amazon Ads dashboard, click on the campaign name, and you'll be taken inside the campaign itself.

You'll be shown a list of the ad groups within your category targeting campaign. As you can see from the screenshot below, I have created six ad groups within this campaign, with each targeting a different category.

Fig. 12.13

To add a new category, simply click on the *Create ad group* button, highlighted below.

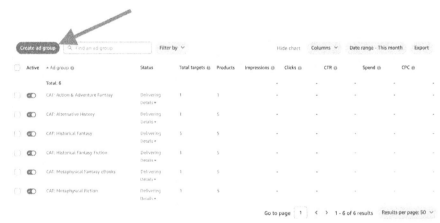

Fig. 12.14

Step 15

Then, just follow the steps we have been through in this chapter to create your additional ad groups:

- Choose the book you'd like to advertise (the same book as you are advertising in the first ad group you created)
- Choose *Product targeting*
- Choose the category you'd like to target
- Set your bid
- Name your ad group

To finish, click the *Create ad group* button at the bottom of the screen and this new ad group will be added into your existing campaign.

Repeat this process until you have a total of three to six ad groups within this single campaign. I wouldn't recommend having more than six because the budget will be spread too thin and you have no control over which ad group the budget is spent on.

If, after five to seven days, you are seeing that some ad groups aren't receiving much in the way of budget, impressions, and clicks, you may need to increase the campaign budget to $15-$20 per day, just to ensure that there is enough budget to go around.

And that wraps up category targeting campaigns, so let's now move on to your Action Steps for Day 3 ...

Action Step for Day 3

Setup Your Discovery Phase Campaigns

G o ahead and follow the instructions over the previous few chapters to set up the following:

- 1 x automatic targeting campaign advertising one book
- 1 x category targeting campaign (with three to six ad groups) advertising the same book as the automatic targeting campaign

Once you have these campaigns set up, you're ready to move on to Day 4 ... the research phase of the Amazon Ads funnel.

Day 4

The Research Phase

P hase two of the Amazon Ads funnel is all about doing your own research, based on what you know about your genre, your comparable (comp) authors, and how readers discover books like yours.

This phase allows you to have much more control over your targeting compared to the automatic and category targeting campaigns you set up in the discovery phase. This also means that it takes a little more upfront work, as well as intuition and knowledge of your genre.

Despite this, the research phase can be a fascinating place to really dive deep into your genre and discover more about your readers.

So, let's jump into it ...

Chapter Thirteen

Manual Targeting

A s I mentioned in the introduction to Day 4, the research phase allows you to have much more control over what you are targeting and where your ads are showing up on Amazon.

We achieve this through the use of manual targeting, which you had a taste of when setting up the category targeting campaign on Day 3.

There are three campaigns we're going to set up together today, that all use manual targeting:

- Author targeting campaign
- Search-term targeting campaign (e.g., crime thrillers, historical fantasies, etc.)
- ASIN targeting campaign (i.e., the ASINs of specific books)

There are two types of manual targeting available with Amazon Ads:

- Keyword targeting
- Product targeting

We used product targeting on Day 3 to set up the category targeting campaign. We'll also be using product targeting to target specific ASINs.

ASIN stands for *Amazon Standard Identification Number.* Every single book on Amazon has its own unique ASIN, and with Amazon Ads, we can show our ads on the product pages of any ASIN of our choosing.

This is the most granular targeting available on Amazon Ads and it can work extremely well. There are a few nuances to keep in mind with ASIN targeting, all of which I'll be covering shortly here on Day 4.

With keyword targeting, we can target specific keywords that relate to our books. However, there's a little more to it than that!

There are three different "match types" we can use with keyword targeting. Match types allow you control over which customer search queries will match (and, therefore, trigger) your chosen keywords to show your ads.

The three match types are:

- Broad match
- Phrase match
- Exact match

Let's explore each of these match types in more detail to help you understand how and when to use each of them, along with some examples to illustrate each of their use cases.

Broad match keywords mean your ad *could* show when someone searches for something that contains all the words within your keyword, in any order, but can also include other words, as well as plurals and synonyms.

EXAMPLE: If you were targeting the keyword historical fantasy *as a broad match keyword, your ad could be shown when someone searches for:*

- *children's fantasy historical*
- *historical fantasy books*
- *historical fiction fantasy*
- *historical fantasy books by Ken Follett*

Phrase match keywords *may* trigger your ad to show when someone types in your keyword, in the same order, but with additional words on either side, including plurals.

EXAMPLE: If you were targeting the keyword murder mystery *in phrase match, your ad could be triggered to show when a customer searches for:*

- *1920s murder mystery novels*
- *murder mystery novels*
- *murder mystery books*
- *murder mystery books for adults*
- *adult murder mystery books*

Exact match keywords do exactly what they say on the tin! A customer search term has to *exactly* match your keyword in order for your ad to trigger; no additional words can be used, but plurals of your keyword can still trigger your ad to show if you are using the singular version, and vice versa.

EXAMPLE: If you were targeting the keyword **crime thriller book,** *your ad could be triggered to show ONLY when a customer searches for the following:*

- *crime thriller book*
- *crime thriller books*

Broad match and phrase match keywords work fantastically well in the re-search phase of the Amazon Ads funnel, whereas exact match keywords perform well in the performance phase of the funnel, when we are looking to scale things up. However, if a client has the budget, I will test all three match types in the research phase.

As each match type performs so differently and they play different roles, I never use multiple match types in the same campaign; I always have separate campaigns for each match type.

As we move through the next few chapters, all of this will start to make a lot more sense, particularly when you begin implementing the steps I'm about to share with you in your own Amazon Ads.

So, let's do it!

Chapter Fourteen

Author Targeting

The first campaign we're going to set up in the research phase is an author targeting campaign.

If you haven't already, I highly recommend that you download your FREE Amazon Ads Toolkit, inside of which you will find the Amazon Ads Targeting Tool; the tool I have built and use every single day to help me manage Amazon Ads for authors:

www.matthewjholmes.com/acos

Before we launch our author targeting campaign, we first need to collect the names of authors that are relevant to the book(s) we are advertising.

You may already have a good idea of who these authors are. Even if you do, I still recommend that you follow the steps I'm about to walk you through to discover authors that Amazon deem are relevant to your books.

Step 1

Head on over to your Amazon author page and look down the left-hand side of the screen, where you will see a section titled *Customers Also Bought Items By.*

Fig. 14.1

As the name suggests, these are authors who your readers have also bought books from; therefore, they are going to be highly relevant to your books and *can* work extremely well with Amazon Ads.

I emphasize the word *can*, because nothing is guaranteed in Amazon Ads; but you can't get more relevant than the authors on this list.

Step 2

Add each author name in your *Customers Also Bought Items By* list into the *Targeting [Authors]* sheet of your Amazon Ads Targeting Tool (or your own spreadsheet if you prefer).

Step 3 (Optional)

If you want to target more authors than are in the *Customers Also Bought Items By* list of your author page, head on over to the product page of the book you are advertising with Amazon Ads.

Scroll down the page and look for a section of the page with a carousel of other books titled *Customers who bought this item also bought*.

Fig. 14.2

You can now look through these books knowing that the authors share the same readers as you.

You may find that many of the authors in here were also listed on your author page in the *Customers Also Bought Items By* list, but there will also be authors here that didn't appear in that list.

Either way, if you find some relevant authors in this section of your product page, add them into your spreadsheet.

Step 4

With your list of authors collected, it's now time to set up your first author targeting campaign. So, head on over to your Amazon Ads dashboard and click on the *Create campaign* button, as you've done a few times already now.

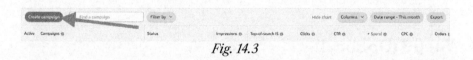

Fig. 14.3

Step 5

Once again, choose the *Sponsored Products* campaign type on the following page.

Choose your campaign type

View drafts

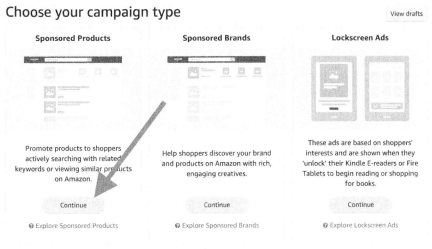

Fig. 14.4

Step 6

We're now going to choose *Standard ad* as the ad format and name our ad group; if you remember, I recommend using the same ad group name for the campaign name (apart from the category targeting campaigns we covered on Day 3). Here's how I name my author targeting ad groups and campaigns:

RESEARCH | [BOOK TITLE] | Authors [BATCH 1]

The reason I add "Batch 1" to the end of the ad group and campaign name is because, over time, I'll be testing many comp authors and I like to keep things as organized as possible.

As I've mentioned a few times already in this book, I don't like using a huge number of keywords/ASINs within a single campaign; smaller numbers of these allows the budget to be spread around more evenly.

With my author targeting campaigns, I target a maximum of 15 authors per campaign. So, if I had 30 authors I wanted to target, for example, I would have two campaigns:

- **RESEARCH | [BOOK TITLE] | Authors [BATCH 1]**
- **RESEARCH | [BOOK TITLE] | Authors [BATCH 2]**

Step 7

Next, choose the book you'd like to advertise in this campaign; this will be the same book you're advertising with the campaigns in the discovery phase of the Amazon Ads funnel.

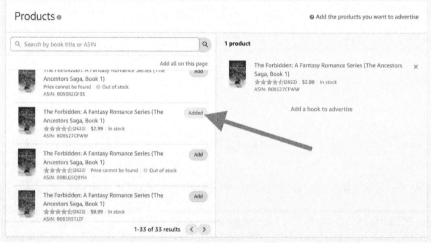

Fig. 14.5

Step 8

Choose *Manual Targeting* and then select *Keyword targeting*, as per the screenshot below. You're getting the hang of this now!

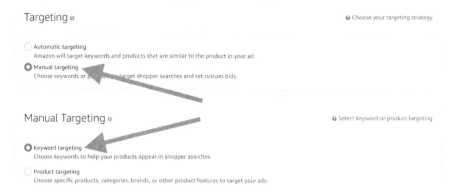

Fig. 14.6

Step 9

Now comes the targeting! This is where all your research and knowledge of your genre comes into play.

You've already collected the author names you'd like to target, so now it's a case of copying them from your spreadsheet and pasting them into the *Keyword targeting* box.

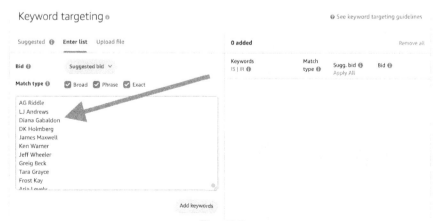

Fig. 14.7

Step 10

Before we add these keywords into the campaign, we need to make a few changes to the settings here.

First of all, the *Bid*. In the drop-down box next to *Bid*, you will see three options to choose from:

- *Suggested bid*
- *Custom bid*
- *Default bid*

Fig. 14.8

I rarely follow Amazon's *Suggested bid* and, instead, prefer to use *Custom bid*, setting it to be fairly aggressive as I want to collect data as quickly as possible. If you have a tight budget, though, and are happy collecting data a little slower, then a lower bid will still work well.

Just remember, as with the previous campaigns we set up on Day 3, if you can, set your bid to at least the minimum of the suggested bid range.

With author targeting campaigns, I typically use a starting bid of $0.78 or, if I'm advertising in a more competitive genre, I'll increase that to $0.88. If that feels too high for you, though, set a bid closer to $0.50, perhaps $0.48 or $0.53.

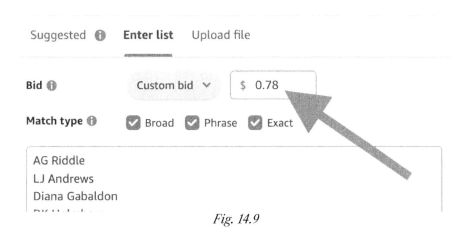

Fig. 14.9

These quirky number bids can just help you beat the competition in the auction as many advertisers bid in $0.05 increments, such as $0.45 or $0.50.

So, choose *Custom bid* from the drop-down *Bid* menu and enter your bid amount. Now it's time to choose the *Match type*.

For author targeting campaigns, I always start with phrase match keywords, as this provides a level of both control and flexibility.

Control in that my ads aren't going to be triggered for any author whose name is Ken if I'm targeting Ken Follett, which could happen if I were using broad match keywords.

And flexibility in that if someone searches for "books by Ken Follett," my ads could still be triggered, which wouldn't be the case were I using exact match keywords.

So, make sure only *Phrase* is selected as the match type by unchecking *Broad* and *Exact*. Then, click *Add keywords* underneath the text box that contains your target author names.

Fig. 14.10

Step 11

Over in the right-hand column, you'll now see your keywords, which have been successfully added into your campaign, along with three other columns:

- *Match type*
- *Sugg. bid* (suggested bid)
- *Bid*

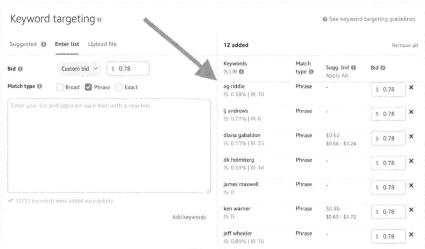

Fig. 14.11

The *Sugg. bid* you see next to some keywords is based on what other advertisers are bidding on the keywords you've chosen; however, it's not 100% accurate, so don't put too much weight behind it.

Below the suggested bid, next to each keyword, you'll also see the suggested bid range, e.g., *$0.38 - $0.77*. The suggested bid typically falls somewhere in the middle of this range.

If you'd like to tweak the bids for any of your keywords, you can do that here, or you can do it any time after your campaign has been launched, which is exactly what we'll be doing on Day 6 when we begin optimizing campaigns.

Once you're happy with all the bids for each keyword, continue scrolling down the page.

You will see a *Negative targeting* section next, which, at this stage, you can ignore; I don't do any negative targeting with author targeting campaigns until they have collected some data for me to work with.

Step 12

Next, it's time to choose your bidding strategy. As we covered on Day 3, if you want to be aggressive with your bidding, choose *Fixed bids,* which will spend your money much faster and allow you to collect data quicker, but it may not necessarily turn into sales. It might, but you take a greater risk.

If you want to be a little more conservative and careful with your ad spend, choose *Dynamic bids – down only.*

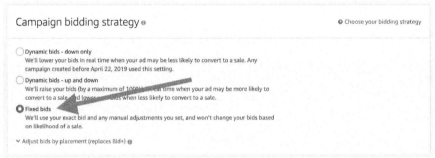

Fig. 14.12

I generally use *Fixed bids* when starting new author targeting campaigns and then switch to *Dynamic bids – down only* after a week or two once I have some good data to work with.

The choice is yours ...

Step 13

On to the final section of the author targeting campaign setup, and now it's time to name your campaign.

As ever, I use the same name for my campaigns as I do for my ad groups. So, in this case, my campaign name is going to be:

RESEARCH | The Forbidden | Authors [BATCH 1]

Fig. 14.13

Step 14

Next, add your campaign to the relevant *Portfolio*; for me, the *Portfolio* is called *2 | The Forbidden [RESEARCH]*.

Fig. 14.14

Step 15

As before, I leave the *Start* and *End* date as default. With the daily budget for these author targeting campaigns, I like to start at $20 per day.

The reason I use a higher budget on research campaigns is purely because they can convert extremely well; you are targeting highly relevant keywords; and, with relatively high bids, I like to give the campaign enough breathing room to generate at least 20 clicks per day. It may not necessarily achieve 20 clicks, but the budget is available to do so.

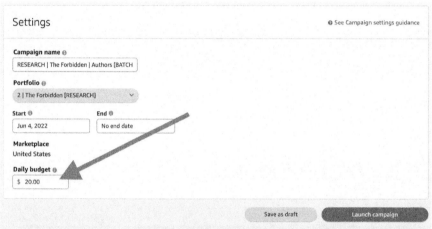

Fig.14.15

Step 16

Finally, review all the information on this page, including the naming conventions you've used, the keywords, the bids, the budget, and the book(s) you are advertising.

Happy? Click the *Launch campaign* button!

If you have more authors you'd like to target, follow the exact same steps we've been through in this chapter and set up another campaign, ensuring that you add [BATCH 2] to the end of the campaign name and ad group name.

Let the campaign run. On Day 6, I'll be showing you how to optimize it.

Coming up next, though, we'll set up a campaign targeting specific search terms related to your book, so when you're ready, I'll see you in the next chapter.

Chapter Fifteen

Search-Term Targeting

We're now moving on to search-term targeting. One question that may be cropping up for you as you read this is, *what is a search term?*

I think of search terms as how readers search for a specific type of book. They aren't looking for a specific author or a specific book title; instead, they are looking for a particular genre of book (fiction), or a book that solves a specific problem (non-fiction).

Let's solidify this with a few examples.

Example #1

If a reader is searching for a mystery book, the search term they type into the Amazon search bar could be:

- mystery books
- mystery novels
- mystery thriller suspense
- mystery thriller
- mystery fiction
- mysteries best sellers
- mystery books best sellers for men

Example #2

If a reader is searching for a crime book set in the UK, the search term they type into the Amazon search bar could be:

- English crime mysteries
- English mystery detective
- British mysteries female
- English police procedurals
- English crime novels
- English mystery novels
- English mystery series
- British crime fiction
- British crime books

Example #3

If a reader is searching for a self-help book about personal growth, the search term they type into the Amazon search bar could be:

- motivation books for men
- achieving goals book
- books for men self-growth
- best self-growth books
- self-growth books paperback
- how to be yourself
- how to master emotions
- improving self-esteem

Search-term targeting is all about putting yourself in your readers' shoes and thinking about what their behaviour could look like if they were looking to read a book like yours; what would they search for to find it?

So, how do you find these search terms? Let's dive into it …

Before we do, however, just as with the author targeting campaigns, I'm looking to use a maximum of 15 search terms per campaign to ensure each search term receives enough budget to be able to prove themselves as a worthy contender for scaling.

Search-Term Research

First of all, make a note of three to five search terms that immediately come to mind when you think of your book. These could even be the keywords you have used in your KDP account when going through the process of publishing your book on Amazon.

Once you have your shortlist of keywords, head on over to the Amazon store where you'll be advertising (e.g., Amazon.com, Amazon.co.uk, etc.) and, from the drop-down box next to the search bar, select *Kindle Store*.

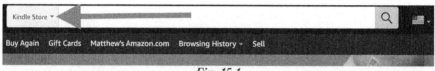

Fig. 15.1

Begin typing the keywords from your shortlist into the search bar, one at a time. When you start typing, you'll see that Amazon will show you suggestions of other keywords you may not have thought of, as you can see from the example below.

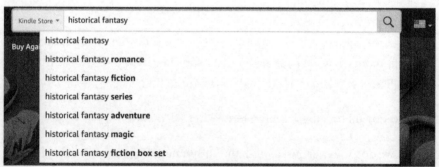

Fig. 15.2

Real people, real customers, and real readers have actually searched for the keywords shown in the drop-down box here on Amazon. Add any of these keywords that apply to your book into your Amazon Ads Targeting Tool.

N.B. There are third-party tools you can use for search term research that can provide even more ideas for you. The only research tool I use and recommend is called Publisher Rocket, created by Dave Chesson and his team over at Kindlepreneur.

On top of the incredible keyword research tool built into Publisher Rocket, it also has many other useful tools that can save you hours of research time and also allows you to discover insights into your genre, your comp authors, and how your readers think when searching for books like yours.

You can find out more and purchase your copy of Publisher Rocket on the link below:

www.matthewjholmes.com/rocket

[Please note that the above link is an affiliate link. If you decide to purchase Publisher Rocket through my link, I may earn a small commission at no additional cost to yourself, which helps to support me put out resources like this book into the hands of authors around the world.]

Completed your search-term research and added the most relevant ones into your Amazon Ads Targeting Tool? Excellent! Let's set up your search-term campaign!

Step 1

You'll be able to do this in your sleep soon! Head on over to your Amazon Ads dashboard and click *Create campaign*.

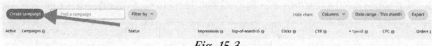

Fig. 15.3

Step 2

Once again, choose the *Sponsored Products* campaign type.

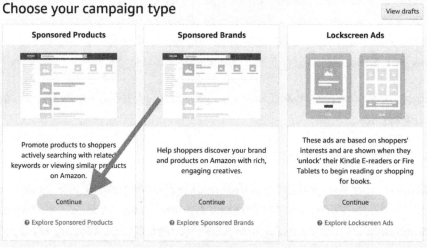

Fig. 15.4

Step 3

To begin the campaign creation process, choose *Standard ad* as the ad format.

Fig. 15.5

Now it's time to name your ad group, which, as I'm sure you've figured out by now, will be the same as your campaign name. Here's how I name my search-term campaigns and ad groups:

RESEARCH | [BOOK TITLE] | Search Terms [BATCH 1] - [MATCH TYPE]

The reason I include the match type in the campaign and ad group name is because, at the research phase, I am testing the same keywords in each match type (broad, phrase, and exact), as they all perform differently and play different roles.

If your budget is tight and you don't have the available cash to test more than one match type at this stage, stick to broad or phrase match.

Personally, if I'm working with a smaller budget, I will start off testing search terms in phrase match.

If, after a week or two, I am not seeing many impressions, clicks, and sales, despite competitive bids, then I will test those same search terms in broad match, which will generate more data for me, but may also create more wasted ad spend by showing my ads for irrelevant search terms.

So, it's important to keep on top of your optimization when running broad match campaigns. Optimization is ***always*** important, whatever type of campaign you're running, but particularly so with broad match campaigns. However, optimization is a topic for another day – Day 6 of this book to be precise!

For now, let's set up this search-term campaign using phrase match keywords; so, our ad group name (and campaign name) will be:

RESEARCH | The Forbidden | Search Terms [BATCH 1] - PHRASE

Step 4

Choose the book you will be advertising in this campaign (the same book as you have used in all the previous campaigns you've launched up to this point).

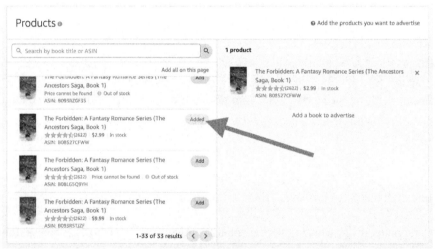

Fig. 15.6

Step 5

Choose *Manual Targeting* and then *Keyword targeting*, just as you did for the author targeting campaign.

Fig. 15.7

Step 6

Scrolling down the page to the *Keyword targeting* section, I recommend setting a custom bid of $0.50 – $0.80. I realise that this is quite a range, but it's very difficult for me to give you an exact bid amount when I don't know your genre.

What I can tell you, though, is that these search-term keywords can be very expensive; I have some clients who are in particularly competitive genres, where a single click can cost $2.50 or higher!

Again, use an irregular number bid, such as $0.53 or $0.67. For this campaign I'm setting up here, I'll be using a bid of $0.88.

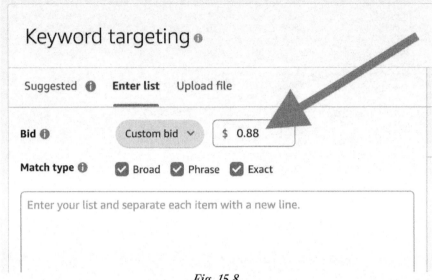

Fig. 15.8

Step 7

Next, choose your *Match type*. As I covered earlier in this chapter, if budget is tight, stick to *Phrase* keywords to begin with, which will give you the best of both worlds, with control over ad spend and flexibility in discovering new search terms.

So, uncheck *Broad* and *Exact* to leave just *Phrase* selected.

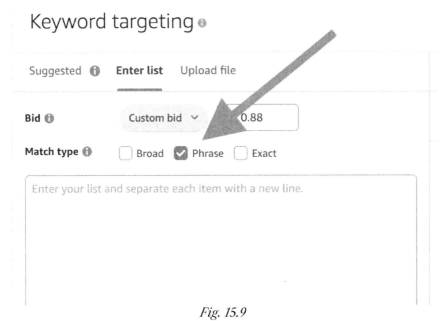

Fig. 15.9

Step 8

Copy and paste the search terms you discovered earlier from your Amazon Ads Targeting Tool into the *Keyword targeting* box and then click *Add keywords* to add them into your campaign.

As I covered at the beginning of this chapter, I like to use a maximum of 15 search terms per campaign.

Fig. 15.10

Step 9

The only negative keyword I add at this stage is the word *free*, as a negative phrase keyword, but ONLY if the book I'm advertising isn't free. Once you have been running campaigns for a few weeks or months, you'll find yourself adding more negative keywords into every new campaign you launch because you will have the data.

Fig. 15.11

In the Amazon Ads Toolkit, I have created a "Negative Keyword List," where you can add your negative phrase and negative exact keywords over time and simply copy and paste them into every new campaign.

Step 10

Next, choose your bidding strategy. As search terms can be very competitive, I like to start these campaigns using *Fixed bids*.

However, as I've covered a few times throughout the book so far, this is a more aggressive approach, and if you're not comfortable using *Fixed bids*, choose *Dynamic bids – down only* instead.

Fig. 15.12

Step 11

On to the final stage of the campaign setup now:

- Copy and paste your ad group name into the *Campaign name* box
- Add this campaign into the relevant *Portfolio*
- Leave the *Start* and *End* date as default

- Set a *Daily budget* (I like to start with $20 per day, but use a lower budget if this is too high for you)

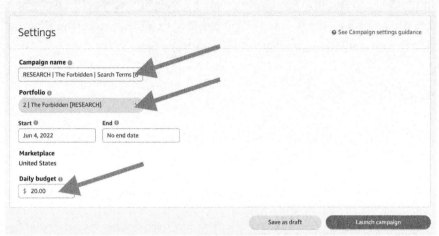

Fig. 15.13

Finally, after checking through all the details you've entered on this page, once you're happy, click the *Launch campaign* button.

If you have more search terms to target and test, follow the steps we've just been through in this chapter and set up another campaign for these additional search terms.

And, if you have the budget, set up two new campaigns using the same search terms you've used in this first campaign, naming the ad groups and campaigns accordingly:

- 1 x campaign for broad match
- 1 x campaign for exact match

When you're ready, let's move on to the final chapter of Day 4, where we'll be setting up an ASIN targeting campaign together.

Chapter Sixteen

ASIN Targeting

A SIN targeting is the most granular targeting available with Amazon Ads. As already mentioned, ASIN stands for *Amazon Standard Identification Number.*

Every single book on Amazon has its own unique ASIN, and with ASIN targeting, you can show your ads on the product pages of the exact books you want to target.

With ASIN targeting, your ads will predominantly appear on product pages, but they can also show on the search result pages when a customer searches for a keyword related to your targeted ASIN.

As you are being so granular and specific with ASIN targeting, the CPCs (costs per clicks) can be expensive.

The CPCs you pay depend on the popularity of the book you're targeting, how much other advertisers are bidding on them, and, although I haven't seen this confirmed by Amazon, I believe that the better a book is ranked in the Amazon Best Seller Rank, the higher the bid required.

The reason I believe this is the case is that the better a book is ranked, the more eyeballs that book product page is going to receive. And with so many readers viewing that product page, competition is going to be fierce to get a piece of that action with Amazon Ads.

Just think, a book positioned at #100 on the Amazon Best Seller Rank on Amazon.com, generates around 1,000 sales per day. The number of readers landing on that book product page, however, is going to be thousands more, because no book has a 100% conversion rate! The average Amazon conversion rate is around 10%-15%, meaning that for every 100 people who visit a product page, only 10-15 of them will make a purchase.

Now you have a better understanding of ASIN targeting and how it works. But before you launch your first ASIN targeting campaign, you need to find some ASINs to target.

The way I like to use ASIN targeting is to find the ASINs of a particular author and target all of their books, or a particular series of theirs if they have written multiple series that perhaps don't all tie in with your books.

The other strategy I use with ASIN targeting is to pick out the top 10 books in a relevant category that your book is listed in, such as women's detective fiction.

Let's begin then ...

Collecting ASINs of Other Authors

We'll start by collecting the ASINs of your comp authors. To help make this process as efficient as possible, I recommend you download the Amazon Ads Targeting Tool, included in the Amazon Ads Toolkit, and use the sheet titled "ASIN Targeting" (aptly named, I know!).

In here, you can collect the following information for every book:

- ASIN
- Author name
- Book titles
- Series title (if applicable)

Although we'll only be using the ASINs in the ASIN targeting campaign, it's useful to collect the other information about each book, as you never know when it may come in handy.

Step 1

Head on over to the author page of a comp author of yours. For this example, I'm going to use E.E. Holmes (no relation to myself or my wife, Lori!) as she is a good comp author for my wife's books.

Fig. 16.1

Step 2

Scroll down to the books listed on their author page and click on the first one in the list.

Fig. 16.2

Step 3

Once you are on the product page for this book, scroll on down to the *Product details* section.

Product details

ASIN : B00DPN1SNW

Publisher : Lily Faire Publishing; 1st edition (June 28, 2013)

Publication date : June 28, 2013

Language : English

File size : 1466 KB

Text-to-Speech : Enabled

Screen Reader : Supported

Enhanced typesetting : Enabled

X-Ray : Enabled

Word Wise : Enabled

Print length : 271 pages

Lending : Not Enabled

Best Sellers Rank: #3,451 in Kindle Store (See Top 100 in Kindle Store)

    #1 in Teen & Young Adult Ghost Stories eBooks

    #1 in Occult Astral Projection

    #3 in Occult Ghosts & Haunted Houses

Customer Reviews: ⭐⭐⭐⭐☆ ˅   6,327 ratings

Fig. 16.3

Step 4

What you're looking for here is the ASIN number, which you can find right at the top of the *Product details* section, as highlighted below.

Product details

ASIN : B00DPN1SNW

Publisher : Lily Faire Publishing; 1st edition (June 28, 2013)

Publication date : June 28, 2013

Language : English

File size : 1466 KB

Text-to-Speech : Enabled

Screen Reader : Supported

Enhanced typesetting : Enabled

X-Ray : Enabled

Word Wise : Enabled

Print length : 271 pages

Lending : Not Enabled

Best Sellers Rank: #3,451 in Kindle Store (See Top 100 in Kindle Store)

　　#1 in Teen & Young Adult Ghost Stories eBooks

　　#1 in Occult Astral Projection

　　#3 in Occult Ghosts & Haunted Houses

Customer Reviews: ☆☆☆☆☆ ⌄   6,327 ratings

Fig. 16.4

Copy and paste this ASIN in to your Amazon Ads Targeting Tool. Next, go ahead and copy and paste the book title, author name and series title as well.

Collecting ASINs of the Top 10 Books in Your Category

When collecting ASINs from the categories your books are listed in, you need to be aware that there could be books in these categories that don't belong there.

The books have either been placed there automatically by Amazon or authors have chosen to list their books in categories that are potentially easier to rank in the top 100 and achieve the coveted "best seller" tag on their books.

As with everything in Amazon Ads, always keep *relevance* top of mind when deciding which ASINs to target.

Step 1

Head over to the book product page of the book you will be advertising and scroll on down to the *Product details* section.

What you're looking for here are the three categories underneath the *Best Sellers Rank*, as highlighted in the screenshot below.

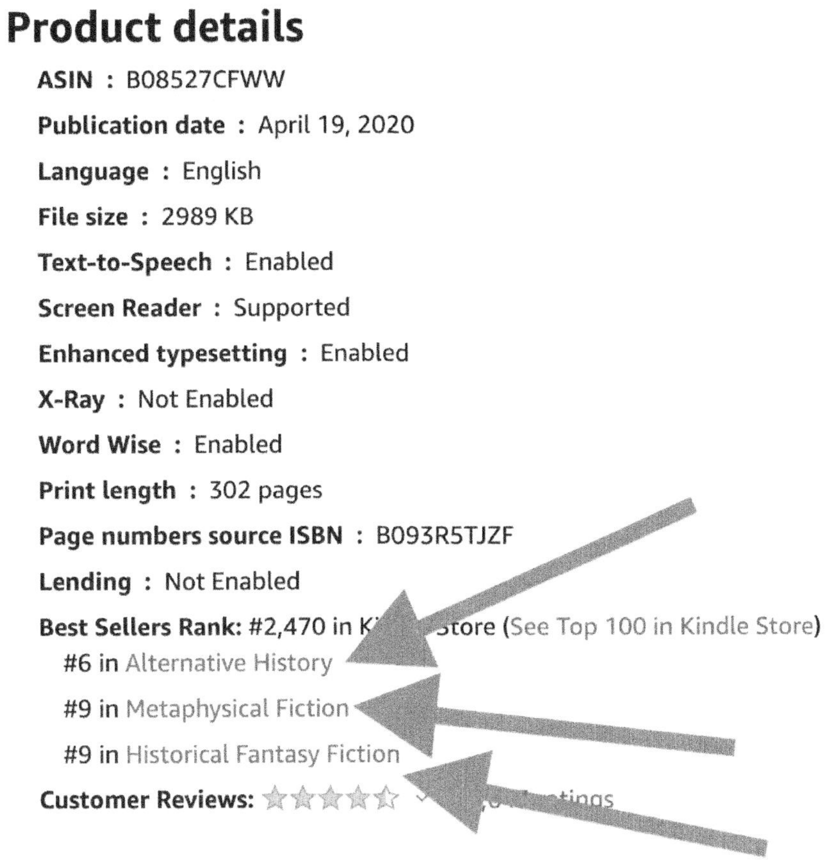

Product details

ASIN : B08527CFWW

Publication date : April 19, 2020

Language : English

File size : 2989 KB

Text-to-Speech : Enabled

Screen Reader : Supported

Enhanced typesetting : Enabled

X-Ray : Not Enabled

Word Wise : Enabled

Print length : 302 pages

Page numbers source ISBN : B093R5TJZF

Lending : Not Enabled

Best Sellers Rank: #2,470 in K   Store (See Top 100 in Kindle Store)
   #6 in Alternative History
   #9 in Metaphysical Fiction
   #9 in Historical Fantasy Fiction
Customer Reviews: ☆☆☆☆☆   tings

Fig. 16.5

Click on one of these categories and you'll be taken to the top 100 list of books in that category.

Fig. 16.6

Step 2

Scroll through the top 100 list, looking for books that are relevant to your book. Click on them, check the description, and, if it's relevant, copy and paste the ASIN, author name, book title and series title into your Amazon Ads Targeting Tool on the sheet titled "Top 10 ASINs."

The process of collecting ASINs can take 10 minutes, or it can take 10 hours! Don't think you need to collect thousands of ASINs today; give yourself 10 minutes, if that's all the time you have, collect 10-15 ASINs, and launch the campaign I'm about to walk you through.

Collecting ASINs (and keywords for that matter) is going to be an ongoing process; it will become part of your routine when managing your Amazon Ads. Over time, you will start to build up a library of ASINs to test.

Launch Your ASIN Targeting Campaign

With your ASINs collected, let's now dive in and set up your ASIN targeting campaign.

Step 1

As you have done a few times now, head over to your Amazon Ads dashboard and click *Create campaign*

Fig. 16.7

.

Step 2

You'll be doing this with your eyes closed soon! Choose the *Sponsored Products* campaign type, as you've done several times now!

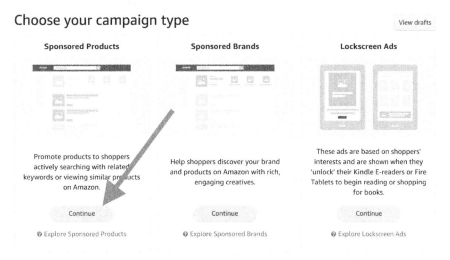

Fig. 16.8

Step 3

Once again, choose *Standard ad* as the ad format.

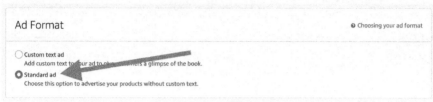

Fig. 16.9

Now it's time to name the ad group, which, as before, will also be the name of our campaign. Here's how I name my ASIN targeting campaigns:

RESEARCH | [BOOK TITLE] [TARGET AUTHOR NAME] ASINs

To put this into context, here's what I'll be using in this example as we set up the ASIN targeting campaign together:

RESEARCH | The Forbidden | EE Holmes ASINs

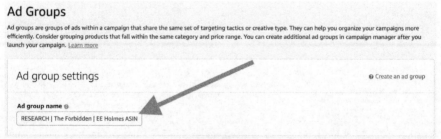

Fig. 16.10

Step 4

Choose the book you'd like to advertise in this campaign; as in all the other campaigns you've launched up to this point, make sure you are advertising the same book in each campaign, otherwise the Amazon Ads funnel we're building here won't be working to its full potential.

Fig. 16.11

Step 5

When you reach the *Targeting* settings, choose *Manual targeting* and then select *Product targeting*.

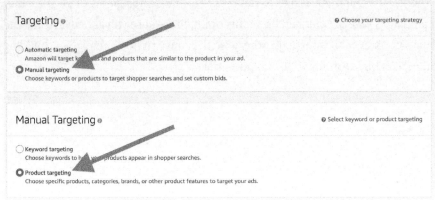

Fig. 16.12

Step 6

Continue scrolling down to the *Product targeting* settings and, here, instead of *Categories*, as we used back on Day 3, today, we need to click the *Individual products* tab.

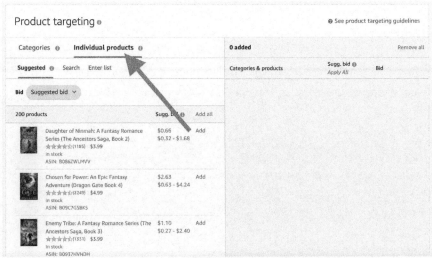

Fig. 16.13

Step 7

You may see a list of suggested ASINs here, some of which could be your own books. From my experience, these suggested ASINs don't work overly well in most cases; personally, I prefer hand-picking the ASINs I want to target. To do that, we're going to click on the *Enter list* option.

Fig. 16.14

Step 8

Next, before we enter the list of ASINs, we need to choose a *Bid*.

As we have done in the previous manual targeting campaigns, I prefer to set a *Custom bid* across all the targets within a specific campaign and then adjust the bids accordingly over time based on the performance of each target.

With ASIN targeting, as I mentioned at the beginning of this chapter, in most instances, you will need to bid fairly high to gain any sort of traction. So, I like to start bids for ASIN targeting campaigns around $0.80 – $0.90. So, for this example, I'll be using a *Custom bid* of $0.88. If that feels too high for you, though, choose a lower bid to begin with and adjust accordingly.

Fig. 16.15

Step 9

Now it's time to enter the ASINs you collected earlier into the text box of the *Product targeting* section. Once entered, click the *Target* button.

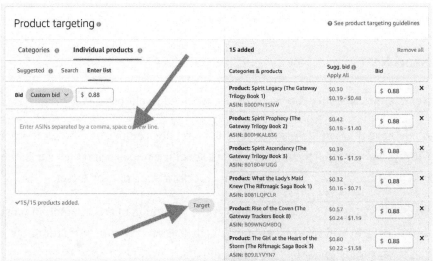

Fig. 16.16

Your chosen ASINs will then be added into this campaign. You can adjust the bids of each ASIN here if required based on what you are seeing with the suggested bid range next to each targeted ASIN.

Step 10

There's no need to do any negative targeting with an ASIN targeting campaign, because our ads will only be shown on the ASINs you've just added, so you can scroll right past this section without stopping.

The penultimate step of the ASIN targeting campaign is the *Campaign bidding strategy*.

As ASIN targeting can be highly competitive, I like to use the *Fixed bids* bidding strategy with these campaigns, to ensure that Amazon is taking my full bid into account and isn't adjusting it in any way (up or down) based on its knowledge of the book I'm advertising. However, if this feels too aggressive for you, start with *Dynamic bids – down only* instead.

Fig. 16.17

Step 11

The final stage of setting up your ASIN targeting campaign is the campaign settings themselves:

- *Campaign name* (the same as the ad group name)
- Choose the relevant *Portfolio* (research)
- Leave the *Start* and *End* date as default
- Choose your *Daily budget* (I recommend $20 if you can, otherwise, a minimum of $10 per day)

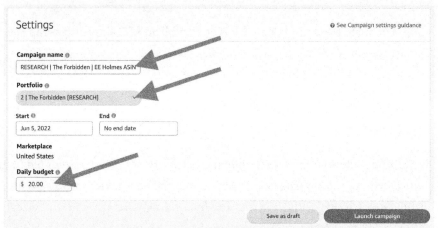

Fig. 16.18

Step 12

Take a final check over everything on this page to ensure all the details are correct, you're advertising the right book, etc. and, once you're happy, click the *Launch campaign* button.

And that, as they say, is that! We'll call that a wrap for Day 4. Congratulations!

Make sure you complete the Action Step for today, which, you've probably guessed by now, is building out the three campaigns we've covered over the past few chapters.

Once these campaigns are set up, it's time to move on to Day 5 ... the performance phase of the Amazon Ads funnel.

Action Step for Day 4

Set Up Your Research Campaigns

To finish off Day 4, it's now time to go ahead and build out the three research campaigns we've been through:

- 1 x author targeting campaign
- 1 x search-term targeting campaign
- 1 x ASIN targeting campaign

As I've shared with you over the past few chapters, I recommend using a maximum of 15 targets per campaign in the research phase. If you have more than 15 author names, search terms and ASINs you'd like to target, feel free to set up multiple campaigns.

Day 5

The Performance Phase

We've reached the final stage of the Amazon Ads funnel ... the performance phase.

Before we dive in, however, it's important to understand that you won't be starting any campaigns in the performance phase until your research and discovery campaigns have been running for at least a week or two, minimum.

The reason being, if you remember back to Day 1 where we covered the Amazon Ads funnel, is that we are moving proven keywords and ASINs from the discovery and research campaigns into the relevant performance campaigns.

Amazon Ads take time to start delivering, collecting the relevant data, and making sales. I like to wait at least a week or two for these initial campaigns to start generating the data I need to make strategic decisions.

If you're spending hundreds of dollars per day, it is possible to collect this data in as little as a week. If you're spending $10 per day, however, then you could be waiting two to four weeks before you have enough data to start the performance phase campaigns.

We'll be covering in this chapter the performance campaigns you'll be setting up once you have the required data, as well as the thresholds I work to when deciding which keywords and ASINs to move from the discovery and research campaigns into the required performance campaign.

With these disclaimers out of the way, let's move into the performance phase of the Amazon Ads funnel ...

Chapter Seventeen

Scaling What Works

You may have heard rumors that Amazon Ads are hard to scale. And those rumors would be true! Amazon Ads *are* hard to scale. And don't be surprised if your ads don't spend the full daily budget you allocated to them.

Scaling Amazon Ads is a gradual process. Yes, you could scale rapidly and rush the process, but you run the high risk of scaling what *isn't* working, rather than what *is* working.

As we covered back on Day 2, I work with the 80/20 rule when managing Amazon Ads, meaning that I only want to scale the 20% of keywords and ASINs that are generating 80% of the sales and page reads.

How Do You Classify a Keyword or ASIN That "Works"?

Great question!

To keep things as simple and straightforward as possible, I use a threshold of two or more sales/borrows, meaning that I'm only going to move keywords and ASINs from the research and discovery campaigns into the relevant performance campaign when they have generated at least two sales or borrows in their source campaign.

One sale and/or borrow could be a fluke! While two sales and/or borrows could still potentially be a fluke, I feel a lot more confident in these targets because more than one person has converted into a sale or borrow from the same keyword or ASIN.

You still need to use your common sense when deciding which keywords and ASINs to graduate into the performance phase, and make sure that they are relevant to the book you're advertising.

If targets you're considering moving into the performance phase aren't relevant in any way, shape, or form (which can happen, particularly with automatic targeting campaigns), then they aren't going to scale well at all and you're better off leaving them alone.

Where Do You Find the Keywords and ASINs to Scale?

Finding the keywords and ASINs to scale can be done in a couple of different ways. When starting out, the simplest way is to look into each of your research and discovery campaigns one by one, which I'll be showing you how to do shortly.

The other method of finding these keywords and ASINs is to use the Amazon Ads reports; these are essentially spreadsheets that you download from your Amazon Ads account and open up in spreadsheet software such as Google Sheets, Excel or Numbers.

Diving into the spreadsheets in enough detail to make it worth your while would turn this into an extremely long-winded book!

Instead, I'll be showing the quickest and simplest way to find these keywords and ASINs to scale, without leaving your Amazon Ads account. Sound good? Let's go ...

IMPORTANT: Before we dive in, remember that this is the process you'll be following once your campaigns have been running for at least a week or two and have generated some sales and/or page reads.

Step 1

In your Amazon Ads dashboard, open up the discovery portfolio you created earlier and click on the automatic targeting campaign.

Fig. 17.1

Step 2

Once you're inside the campaign, you'll see a few different options down the left-hand side of your screen:

- *Ad groups:* You set these up when you launched your auto campaign
- *Placements:* This is where you can see which placements your ads are appearing in across Amazon and how each of them is performing. You can also influence your bids on a per-placement basis (e.g., bid an additional 100% on top of your base bid to appear at the top of the search results)
- *Negative targeting:* Negating keywords and ASINs (I do this at the ad group level, NOT the campaign level)
- *Budget rules:* Allow Amazon to adjust your campaign budgets based on performance or a specific event or dates (e.g., Black Friday)
- *Campaign settings:* Adjust campaign name, budget, portfolio, schedule and bidding strategy
- *History:* Review all the changes that have been made to this campaign at the campaign level

To find the keywords and ASINs that we can potentially scale, we need to dive into the next level down, the ad group, so, click on the ad group of this campaign, as highlighted below.

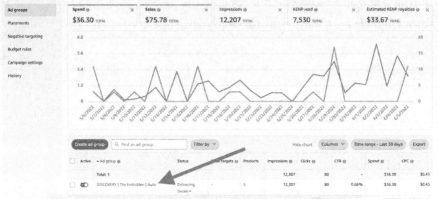

Fig. 17.2

Step 3

Inside the ad group, you will see a new menu down the left-hand side of the screen:

- *Ads:* The books that are being advertised within this ad group
- *Targeting:* The keywords, ASINs, categories or targeting groups you are targeting in this ad group
- *Negative targeting:* Add negating keywords and ASINs to this ad group
- *Search terms:* The keywords and ASINs that have triggered your ad to show (generating impressions, clicks, sales, and page reads)
- *Ad group settings:* Adjust the ad group name and the default bid
- *History:* Review all the changes that have been made to this ad group at the ad group level

When we're looking for keywords and ASINs to scale up, we need to click on the *Search terms* option in the menu.

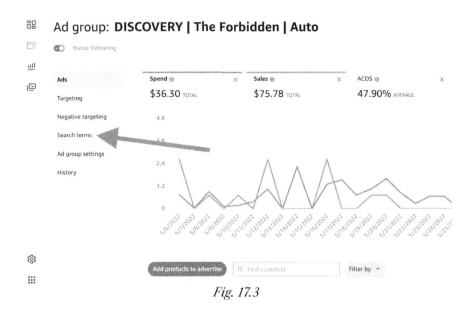

Ad group: **DISCOVERY | The Forbidden | Auto**

Status: Delivering

Ads	Spend ⓘ	×	Sales ⓘ	×	ACOS ⓘ	×
Targeting	$36.30 TOTAL		$75.78 TOTAL		47.90% AVERAGE	
Negative targeting						
Search terms						
Ad group settings						
History						

Add products to advertise   Q Find a product   Filter by ⌄

Fig. 17.3

Step 4

This table you see now will show you the *Customer search terms* (that real people have typed into the Amazon search bar) and ASINs that have generated impressions, clicks, orders, and page reads of the book(s) you're advertising in this ad group.

Ad group: **DISCOVERY | The Forbidden | Auto**

Status: Delivering

Q Find a search term   Filter by ⌄   Columns ⌄   Date range - Last 30 days   Export

Ads									
Targeting	Customer search term ⓘ	Impressions ⓘ	Clicks ⓘ CTR ⓘ	Spend ⓘ	CPC ⓘ	Orders ⓘ	Sales ⓘ	KENP read ⓘ	Estimat
Negative targeting	Total: 41	567	78 13.76%	$35.32	$0.45	22	$75.78	7,576	
Search terms	adventure kindle m/m	1	1 100.00%	$1.24	$1.24	-	-	-	
Ad group settings	ancestor saga series	1	1 100.00%	$0.44	$0.44	-	-	-	
History	ancestors saga	19	2 10.53%	$0.51	$0.26	-	-	1,789	
	ancestors saga book 2	2	1 50.00%	$0.34	$0.34	-	-	-	
	ancestors saga series	9	3 33.33%	$1.31	$0.44	1	$2.99	-	
	ASIN: B01DNN61LB Four Nails, History's Smallest Elephant and I...	5	1 33.33%	$0.12	$0.12	-	-	-	

Fig. 17.4

Before we dive into this data, there's one more step to take ... adjust the time period.

Amazon stores this search-term data for a maximum of 65 days; after that, it's gone! So, when looking at this data, we want to look at this maximum period of time, 65 days.

To do this, click on the *Date range* drop-down menu on the top right-hand side of the table, as shown in the screenshot below.

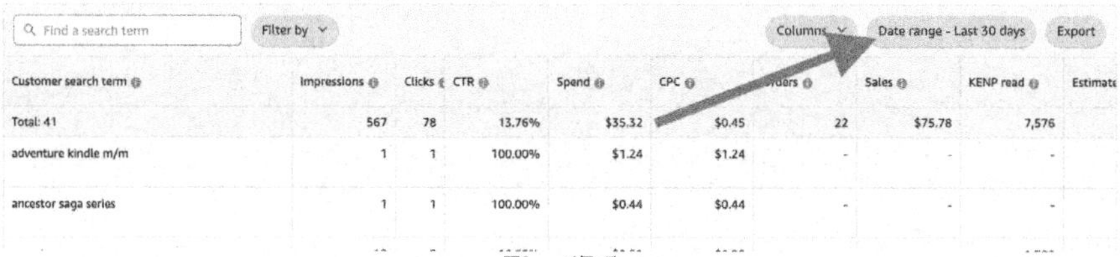

Fig. 17.5

Then, click the *Last 65 days* option in the menu that pops up here.

Fig. 17.6

Step 5

Now we have our 65 days' worth of data here (even if your campaign has only been running for two weeks at this stage, you at least have the maximum amount of data available), it's time to review it and start making some decisions.

I'll now walk you through the step-by-step process I carry out when looking at this data in the Amazon Ads accounts I manage for authors.

If your books are enrolled in Kindle Unlimited, there is an additional step you need to carry out before you review your search terms: finding your Kindle Edition Normalized Page Count (KENPC) for the book you are advertising:

1. Head on over to KDP dashboard bookshelf

2. Click the *Promote and Advertise* button next to the book you are advertising with Amazon Ads

Fig. 17.7

3. Scroll down to the bottom of the *Promote and Advertise* screen to the section titled *Earn royalties from the KDP Select Global Fund*. In here, you will see the following line of text:

Kindle Edition Normalized Page Count (KENPC) v3: [followed by a number – this number is your KENPC]

At the time of writing (June 2022), the KENPC is on v3; you may see a different version, depending on when you are reading this book.

Fig. 17.8

4. Armed with your KENPC (for me, the KENPC is 390) you're now ready to review your search terms. So, head on back into your Amazon Ads account and into the *Search terms* option of the ad group we were in a few moments ago.

Assessing Your Search Terms for Scaling Opportunities

- Sort the data by number of orders, with the largest number at the top (click the *Orders* column twice to do this)
- Assess which customer search terms (ASINs appear in the *Customer search term* column too) have generated two or more orders and add these into the "Proven Targets" sheet in your Amazon Ads Targeting Tool (separate columns for "Proven ASINs" and "Proven Keywords")
- If your books are NOT in Kindle Unlimited, you're done! You have the keywords and ASINs that are in a position to scale in your performance campaigns. **If your books ARE enrolled in Kindle Unlimited, we have a few more steps to go through ...**
- Back in your Amazon Ads account, sort the data in your search terms table by KENP read, with the largest number at the top (again, you'll need to click the *KENP read* column twice to do this)
- For this next step, you'll need to know your KENPC that you found earlier. Got it? Great!

- Look at the KENP read for the first customer search term in your table and divide it by your KENPC. In the case of my wife's books, her KENPC is 390 and the KENP read of the first customer search term here is 3,219. So, I divide 390 into 3,219, which equals 8.25, which I will round down to 8. This is the number of borrows of your book that are attributable to that specific customer search term.
- Find all the customer search terms that have generated at least two or more borrows and add these into the "Proven Keywords" or "Proven ASINs" column in your Amazon Ads Targeting Tool.

Once you have completed this process for the automatic targeting campaign, you'll need to run through it again with your other campaigns in the discovery and research phases of the Amazon Ads funnel.

There could potentially be some customer search terms in this table that aren't doing anything for you, apart from spending money with little to show for it! Don't worry about these for now; we're going to be dealing with them tomorrow, on Day 6.

For now, with your proven keywords and ASINs collected, it's time to put them to work in the performance phase of the Amazon Ads funnel.

Chapter Eighteen

The Performance Phase Campaigns

N ow you've completed the process of finding and collecting the keywords and ASINs to scale up, it's time to launch your performance campaigns.

So, without further ado, let's dive right into it ...

Step 1

As before, head on over to your Amazon Ads dashboard and create a new campaign.

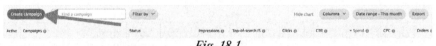

Fig. 18.1

Step 2

Choose the *Sponsored Products* option as the campaign type.

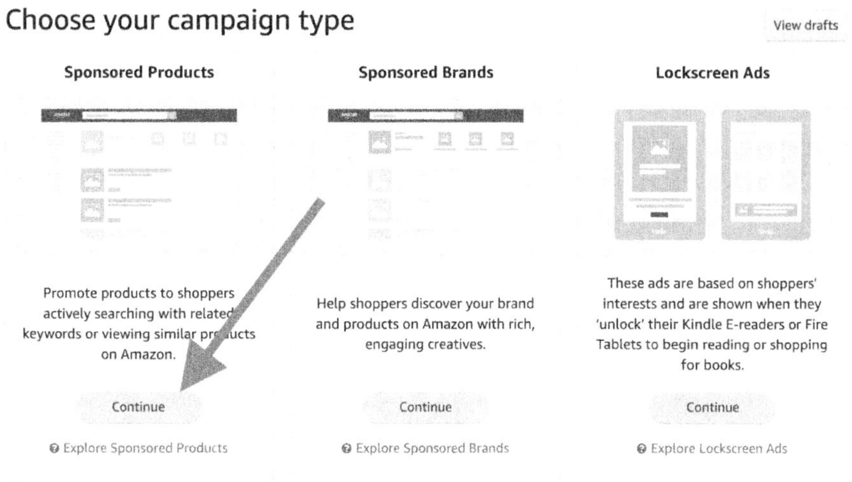

Choose your campaign type

View drafts

Sponsored Products

Sponsored Brands

Lockscreen Ads

Promote products to shoppers actively searching with related keywords or viewing similar products on Amazon.

Help shoppers discover your brand and products on Amazon with rich, engaging creatives.

These ads are based on shoppers' interests and are shown when they 'unlock' their Kindle E-readers or Fire Tablets to begin reading or shopping for books.

Continue

Continue

Continue

❷ Explore Sponsored Products

❷ Explore Sponsored Brands

❷ Explore Lockscreen Ads

Fig.18.2

Step 3

Choose standard ad as the ad format and name your ad group; here's an example of how I name my performance campaigns:

PERFORMANCE | The Forbidden | Proven Keywords

Step 4

Choose the book you will be advertising in this campaign (the same book that has been used in the discovery and research phases)

Fig. 18.3

Step 5

Next, select *Manual Targeting* and, for this first campaign, we're going to be using *Keyword targeting*.

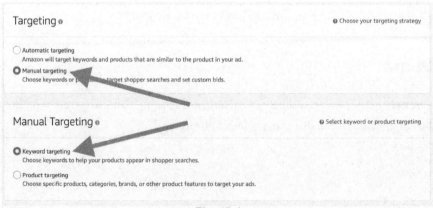

Fig. 18.4

Step 6

In the *Keyword targeting* section, click *Enter list*, then select *Custom bid* from the drop-down menu and deselect *Broad* and *Phrase*, leaving only the *Exact* option selected.

We are using exact match keywords in the performance campaign because we have already done the testing through broad and/or phrase match keywords; we now know what works, so we are doubling down on those keywords by not allowing Amazon to match our proven keywords with other words, which is what they will do with broad and phrase match keywords.

Exact match keywords are the best option for scaling up. Broad and phrase match keywords are predominantly for research purposes.

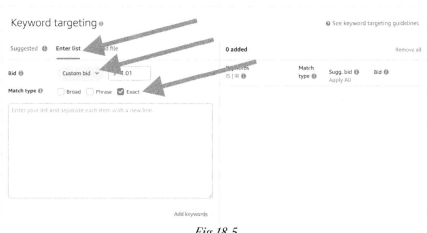

Fig.18.5

Step 7

Copy and paste the keywords from the proven keywords column in your Amazon Ads Targeting Tool into the *Keyword targeting* box in your Amazon Ads campaign setup.

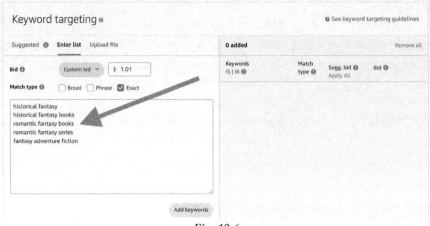

Fig. 18.6

Step 8

Before you add these keywords into your campaign, we need to decide on a bid for each of them. I like to set a *Custom bid* for all the keywords first, then adjust each of them accordingly afterwards – but that's just me!

When scaling up keywords and ASINs, you need to make sure that your bid is considerably higher than the cost per click (CPC) was in the research or discovery campaign where that keyword or ASIN came from. You can find this data back in the search term report of the relevant campaign. Or maybe you know it already, in which case, enter your *Custom bid* now!

The CPC of my keywords in the automatic targeting campaign was, on average, around $0.45 and had a maximum bid of $0.58, so, in this instance, I'm going to set a *Custom bid* in the performance campaign of $0.93.

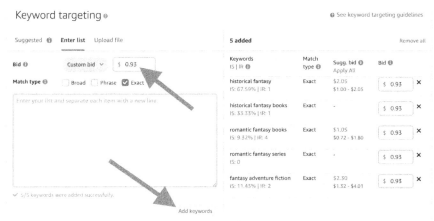

Fig. 18.7

Step 9

As we are using exact match keywords, there is no need to add any negative keywords into this campaign. So, scroll on down to the *Campaign bidding strategy* section, where we are going to select *Fixed bids*.

Fig. 18.8

If there's any campaign where fixed bids are going to be used, at least initially, it's the performance campaigns. We know these keywords work as they have already proven themselves in the research or discovery phases.

At the time of writing, Amazon's algorithm doesn't count a borrow as a conversion. If we were using dynamic bids – down only and Amazon felt a click on one of our proven keywords would not result in a sale (conversion), then it would lower our bid automatically.

However, some of our proven keywords have only generated page reads in the source campaign they came from, not sales. With this in mind, Amazon may lower our bid on a keyword, even if it could result in a borrow followed by page reads, because the Amazon Ads algorithm, at this stage, doesn't see a borrow as a conversion.

This is why I prefer to use fixed bids; it prevents Amazon from fiddling with our bids when a click could convert into a borrow, but not a sale. Fixed bids, as we covered earlier, will ensure that your full bid is taken into account in the Amazon Ads auction.

Step 10

Finally, it's time to enter the campaign *Settings* for your keyword performance campaign, as follows:

- *Campaign name* (same as ad group name)
- *Portfolio* (the performance portfolio you set up on Day 2)
- *Start* and *End* date (leave as default)
- *Daily budget* (I like to start with a $30 per day budget on performance campaigns and adjust up or down from there)

Fig. 18.9

Once you've completed the campaign *Settings*, review all the information you've entered into this campaign so far and, when you're ready, click the *Launch campaign* button.

With your proven keywords campaign complete, run through the step-by-step process we've just been through and create your proven ASINs campaign, using the proven ASINs you added into your Amazon Ads Targeting Tool.

Just make sure that you are using product targeting instead of keyword targeting when you are setting up your campaign (if you need a reminder on setting up an ASIN targeting campaign, refer back to Day 4, Chapter 16).

Well, that is going to wrap up Day 5, and with it the Amazon Ads funnel. You've built out the core campaigns, so now it's time to let the data roll in.

Tomorrow, Day 6, we're going to look at what to do with this data to make your ad spend as efficient as possible by, once again, focusing on the 80/20 and also reducing any wastage as much as possible.

Action Step for Day 5

Set Up Your Performance Campaigns

A s I covered at the beginning of Day 5, there's no need to set up the performance campaigns until you have some keywords and ASINs to put into them, which, depending on how much you're spending, could be a week or two after setting up your discovery and research campaigns, or it could be 2-4 weeks.

In the meantime, if your research and discovery campaigns are still collecting data, start making a habit of looking at the search terms for each campaign, as we've covered here on Day 5.

Begin to familiarize yourself with how your readers are looking for and discovering your books. It's amazing what you learn when you see this data, and you start to see how it can influence new campaigns and give you new targeting ideas for your Amazon Ads.

When you have the data ready and you have keywords and ASINs with more than two sales and/or borrows, set up the two performance campaigns:

- 1 x proven keywords campaign
- 1 x proven ASINs campaign

And with that, let's move on to Day 6 ... Optimization for Growth.

Day 6

Optimization for Growth

J ust letting your ads run wild is going to hurt your profitability and results in the long term.

Conversely, however, fiddling with your ads too much can also have a negative impact on your results.

So, today, we are going to be finding that balance between the two and discussing how to optimize your Amazon Ads.

Chapter Nineteen

The Amazon Ads Dashboard and Key Metrics

A s an author, numbers, and analysis of those numbers, may not always come naturally to you.

However, when it comes to the numbers involved with your Amazon Ads, we are talking about your money, so you naturally start thinking about things a bit differently; especially if your goal is to earn a full-time living from your writing.

You would have seen the Amazon Ads dashboard as you've been setting up your campaigns in the previous chapters. In this chapter, I'm going to dive into all the different facets of the dashboard to help you really understand what all those numbers actually mean and how you can use them to optimize your Amazon Ads.

The Amazon Ads dashboard is quirky to say the least, and, unfortunately, doesn't tell you the whole story about the health of your ads.

Here's the main data that is missing from Amazon Ads dashboard:

- How many of your other books have sold/had page reads *because* of your ads (i.e., which campaigns have attributed to sales/page reads of your other books)
- Number of borrows (readers who have borrowed your book as part of their Kindle Unlimited subscription – we have to calculate this manually, and even then, it's a bit of an estimate)
- Royalties received from your campaigns (you only see the numbers based on the sale price of your book, *not* the royalties you receive as the author)

But it's not all bad news. There is some extremely useful data in the dashboard that we can analyze to create new, more profitable campaigns moving forwards, as well as optimize existing campaigns with. For example:

- Impressions
- Clicks
- Click-through rate (CTR)
- Cost per click (CPC)
- Orders (number of books sold)
- Kindle Edition Normalized Pages (KENP Read) – only applicable to authors with books enrolled in Kindle Unlimited
- Estimated KENP royalties – only applicable to authors with books enrolled in Kindle Unlimited

And we can look at these pieces of data on portfolio, campaign, and ad group levels, as well as on an individual target level (i.e., keywords, ASINs, etc.)

So, let's now dive into the Amazon Ads dashboard and decipher some of the numbers you're seeing.

Setting Up Your Dashboard Columns

By default, the Amazon Ads dashboard is missing some of the crucial data we've just been through. The default settings for the columns you'll see in your dashboard are:

- Status
- Type
- Start date
- End date
- Budget
- Spend
- Orders
- Sales
- ACOS

- KENP read

If you're struggling for viewable space on your computer and have to keep scrolling left to right to see all the data, you can choose to switch off some columns.

Here are the columns I have set up on my Amazon Ads dashboards:

- Campaigns (you can't turn this off)
- Status (you can't turn this off)
- Campaign bidding strategy (not currently available in portfolio view)
- Start date
- Impressions
- Clicks
- CTR
- Spend
- CPC
- Orders
- Sales
- KENP read (you can leave this column off if your books aren't in Kindle Unlimited)
- Estimated KENP royalties (you can leave this column off if your books aren't in Kindle Unlimited)

The more time you spend in your Amazon Ads dashboard, the more likely you are to find your own way of setting it up, but I recommend starting with a setup like mine initially and adjust accordingly from there.

So, how do you customize the data you see on your Amazon Ads dashboard? Let's do this together:

1. Click the gray *Columns* drop-down box on the top right of your dashboard and choose *Customise columns*

Fig. 19.1

2. In the pop-up box that appears, tick the box next to the relevant information you want to include on your dashboard. Then click the *Apply* button.

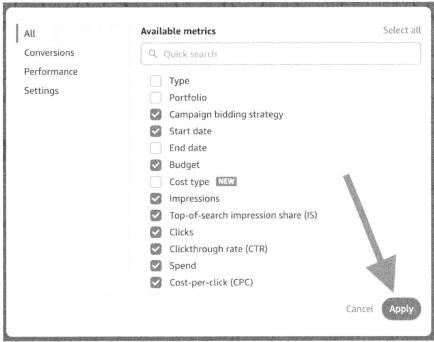

Fig. 19.2

Setting the Date Range

The next important setting is the *Date range*. I've had a few hairy moments when I thought I'd spent hundreds or thousands of dollars in a single day, only to find that I hadn't set this correctly, and the dashboard was showing me data for the past 30 days, rather than just the day before!

To look at data from a particular date range, click the *Date range* box, next to the *Columns* box you clicked when setting up your dashboard columns.

Fig. 19.3

At this stage your campaigns may only have been running for a few days. Once they've been up and running for several weeks or months, however, you'll be coming back to this *Date range* setting a lot to compare how your ads have been performing over different time periods.

Typically, I like to set the *Date range* to *Last 30 days*, as I can see how my campaigns have been performing over a longer period of time.

If I want to drill down into more recent performance of my campaigns, I'll set it to *Last 7 days* or *This week*, or even individual days.

Today				May 2022								June 2022				
Yesterday	<														>	
Last 7 days		Su	Mo	Tu	We	Th	Fr	Sa	Su	Mo	Tu	We	Th	Fr	Sa	
This week		1	2	3	4	5	6	7				1	2	3	4	
Last week		8	9	10	11	12	13	14	5	6	7	8	9	10	11	
Last 30 days		15	16	17	18	19	20	21	12	13	14	15	16	17	18	
This month		22	23	24	25	26	27	28	19	20	21	22	23	24	25	
Last month		29	30	31					26	27	28	29	30			
Year to date																
Lifetime												Cancel		Save		
America/Los_Angeles																

Fig. 19.4

As you can see from the screenshot above, Amazon offers several preset time periods to choose from, or you can use the calendar to select your own time period.

As with the *Columns* setting, you'll find your own rhythm when looking at your data for different *Date ranges*.

Let's now move on to understanding more about the information and numbers you see underneath each column on your Amazon Ads dashboard.

Active

This is simply telling you whether a campaign is switched on or off, indicated by the blue toggle switch.

Campaigns

This is the name of your campaign that you set when creating your ads in the earlier chapters.

Status

This column tells you if your campaign is *Delivering, Paused,* or *Archived*.

Type

This can be either *Sponsored Products Manual Targeting, Sponsored Products Automatic Targeting, Sponsored Brands Manual Targeting* or *Lockscreen Ads Manual Targeting*.

Start and End Date

Quite self-explanatory! The date that your campaign started and the date that it's currently set to end (if at all – you don't need to set an end date on all campaigns).

Budget

The daily budget allocated to this campaign, or the lifetime budget for lockscreen ads, if you've chosen this option.

Spend

How much money you've spent on this campaign (based on date range selected).

Orders

The number of units sold attributed to this ad – this number includes eBooks *and* paperbacks/hardbacks (based on date range selected).

Sales

The amount of money that this ad has generated in your selected date range.

IMPORTANT: This figure is the total amount paid by customers and does not reflect the royalty rate your book falls under. Sales numbers are based on retail price, not royalties received.

For example, if you sold one book at $2.99 with an ad, the sales column would show $2.99. Whereas, the amount you receive as a royalty would be somewhere around $2.03, in most cases, on a 70% royalty rate.

ACOS

ACOS stands for *Advertising Cost of Sale*, but, in my opinion, it isn't overly relevant because it's based on the sales number and doesn't include the KENP royalties reported in your dashboard or any sales or KENP royalties of your other books that came as a result of this campaign (i.e., read-through/sell-through).

And because the number shown in the sales column isn't relevant or accurate as to what you actually receive as a royalty, ACOS is an unreliable data point at this moment in time. This is why I don't even have it in my ads dashboard layout – I pay very little, if any, attention to it!

ACOS is a hotly-debated topic in the Amazon Ads world because it was made for Amazon sellers who sell clothes, toiletries, and anything other than books!

Therefore, ACOS is something you can choose to ignore. Some authors pay attention to it, but personally, I don't. If it's something you feel would benefit you, then by all means use ACOS when analyzing your ads.

Impressions

This indicates how many times your ad has been shown on the Amazon website; that's across search results pages *and* individual book product pages (based on date range selected).

Top-of-Search IS

The percentage of top-of-search impressions this campaign received out of all the top-of-search impressions it was eligible to receive, based on the keywords/ASINs within it (based on date range selected).

Clicks

The number of times your ad has been clicked on (based on date range selected).

Click-Through Rate (CTR)

The ratio, shown as a percentage, of how often your ad has been shown (impressions) divided by the number of clicks your ad has generated (based on date range selected).

The higher the percentage of your CTR, the better. If you can improve your CTR, Amazon will see your campaign as more relevant and *may* therefore reduce the amount you pay every time someone clicks it and show your ad to more readers.

Cost Per Click

How much, on average, you are paying for every click on your ad, in your selected date range. This number is calculated by dividing the number of clicks your ad has generated by the amount you've spent on the ad (over the selected time period).

KENP Read

Only applicable to authors advertising books in Kindle Unlimited, this metric lets you know how many page reads you've had that can be attributed to a particular campaign, within your selected date range.

Keep in mind that, generally, people don't start reading a book they've borrowed in Kindle Unlimited straight away; you will likely see a lag in page reads being attributed to a campaign.

KENP Estimated Royalties

Again, this metric is only applicable to authors advertising books in Kindle Unlimited. It provides you with an estimation of how much you have earned from page reads that can be attributed to an individual campaign, within your selected date range.

This number is only an estimate because the amount Amazon pays authors per page read varies from month to month; typically, however, it sits around $0.0045 per page read.

Actions

The only option here is *Copy*, which allows you to make a carbon copy of an individual campaign.

So that's the different advertising lingo on your Amazon Ads dashboard. The graph at the top of the dashboard will show you a visual representation of the data below, based on the metrics and date range you select.

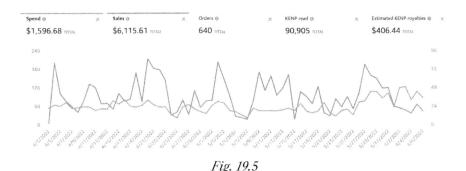

Fig. 19.5

At the time of writing, you can only view five metrics along the top of the graph at any one time and can compare a maximum of two metrics in the graph itself – one metric will display in orange, the other in blue.

To look at any metrics that aren't currently displayed, you'll need to turn one metric off, which you do by clicking the little *X* icon in the corner of the box, as you can see from the screenshot below.

Fig. 19.6

Once you've clicked the *X* icon, you'll see a box labeled *Add metric*, and you'll be able to see a selection of other metrics you can choose to view in the graph.

Fig. 19.7

To select a metric to add to your graph, you just need to click it once.

All of these metrics are available from your main Amazon Ads dashboard, and also when you're looking at ads on a campaign, ad group, and targeting level, which is incredibly useful.

That completes our whistle-stop tour of the Amazon Ads dashboard; in the next chapter, we're going to be diving even deeper into the data to better understand how to optimize your ads, and looking at how individual keywords, products, and categories have performed.

Chapter Twenty

The Issue With ACOS

We've already touched on the term Advertising Cost of Sale (ACOS), and I'm sure you've heard it batted around the author-advertising space. As a reminder, ACOS is calculated as follows:

(Ad spend / Sales) x 100

Essentially, it's a metric that signifies how profitable your Amazon Ads are and it's measured as a percentage. For example, a 25% ACOS is considered excellent in the world of books and signifies a highly profitable campaign.

In short, the lower your ACOS, the more profitable your Amazon Ads are ... THEORETICALLY ...

Here's the kicker though ...

As I mentioned in the previous chapter, if your advertised books are in Kindle Unlimited, the ACOS reported in your Amazon Ads dashboard doesn't take your KENP royalties into account, despite them being tracked within your Amazon Ads dashboard.

On top of that, if you're advertising paperback books, your ACOS will be even more skewed because it is based on the sale price of the advertised book rather than the actual royalty you receive from Amazon for each sale.

So, it's safe to say that the ACOS you see inside your dashboard isn't strictly accurate. Now, don't get me wrong, it's a good indicator for how your ads are doing, but take it with a pinch of salt.

The question then becomes, what should my ACOS be?

If your books are in Kindle Unlimited, you can calculate what I like to call your "Blended ACOS" by using the following calculation:

Ad spend / (Sales + KENP royalties) x 100

This will give you a far more accurate picture of how your Amazon Ads are performing from an ACOS perspective.

I also recommend that you work out your "Breakeven ACOS", which is the ACOS you should be hitting to ensure that your Amazon Ads are earning as much as they are spending.

To work out your breakeven ACOS, you'll need the following information:

- Sale price of book
- Delivery fee or Print cost
- Royalty rate (e.g., 70%)

Let's work out a breakeven ACOS of a book together to put this into some context:

- Sale price of book: $3.99
- Delivery fee: $0.12
- Royalty rate: 70%

We first need to work out our profit margin per sale, which we calculate like this:

(Sale price of book - Delivery fee) x Royalty rate

So, in our example here:

(3.99 - 0.12) x 0.7 = $2.71

So, for each pre-ad profit sale of our book, we earn $2.71. If we spent $2.71 for each sale on Amazon Ads, we would be breakeven. Now we need to calculate our breakeven ACOS as a percentage.

To do that, we simply take our pre-ad profit per sale and divide it by the sale price of the book, which looks like this:

(2.71 / 3.99) x 100 = 67.9%

So, our breakeven ACOS for this book is 67.9%. Remember, this isn't taking any Kindle Unlimited earnings into account, and it's also ignoring any read-through or sell-through to other books in this series or in our catalog/backlist.

When advertising Book 1 of a series, providing you have good read-through/sell-through on that series, you can afford for your ACOS to be higher than the breakeven ACOS you calculate.

The reason for this is that once people have bought Book 1, they are more likely to buy Book 2 organically (i.e., they don't need an ad to remind them to buy Book 2 because they know they want it; and if you've linked to Book 2 at the back of Book 1, they will be able to find it more easily. On a Kindle, Amazon will also push the next book in a series to readers).

I have Amazon Ads accounts I manage where the ACOS is well over 100% and, overall, the author is still making a very healthy profit.

If I were focused on bringing the ACOS down as low as possible, I would need to reduce bids drastically and, therefore, reduce impressions, clicks, sales, and page reads, all of which would have a negative impact on the organic ranking of the book, reducing visibility and all the organic benefits associated with Amazon. Read-through/sell-through to other books in the series or catalog would also suffer when reaching for a low ACOS.

Phew! That was a pretty number-intensive chapter, but hopefully, by now, you can see that focusing on ACOS can actually have a negative impact on your Amazon Ads and that looking at the big picture is a far more healthy and profitable way to assess the performance of your Amazon Ads.

To wrap up this chapter, yes, ACOS is important, but if your books are in Kindle Unlimited particularly, take your ACOS with a pinch of salt.

Instead, make sure you are tracking your Amazon Ads in the Amazon Ads Tracking Tool (included in the Amazon Ads Toolkit) or your own spreadsheet, as well as calculating your blended ACOS within that spreadsheet to make sure it is taking your KENP royalties into account.

Chapter Twenty-one

The Optimization Process

O ptimization will be an ongoing process that is going to make or break the success of your Amazon Ads.

There is a fine balance, however, when it comes to Amazon Ads, between under-optimization and over-optimization.

For me, with accounts I manage that are spending more than $100 per day, I optimize them twice per week. For accounts spending less than $100 per day, I optimize these once per week.

I do, of course, cast my eye over the accounts each day, checking for any red flags or alarm bells that need my attention there and then. When it comes to optimization, however, once or twice a week is ample for most authors.

The best way I feel I can demonstrate the Amazon Ads optimization process is by walking you through how I review and optimize an existing campaign I am managing, which you can then replicate for your own campaigns.

So, let's dive in ...

The campaign I'm going to be optimizing with you in this chapter is an automatic targeting campaign advertising Book 1 in my wife's series, *The Ancestors Saga*.

Step 1

Open the campaign and select a date range of the past 30 days.

Fig. 21.1

Step 2

Click on the ad group, as highlighted below, to dive deeper into what is and isn't working in this campaign.

Fig. 21.2

Step 3

Once inside the ad group, the first thing I do when optimizing an automatic targeting campaign is click the *Targeting* tab in the left-hand menu.

Ad group: **DISCOVERY | The Forbidden | Auto**

Fig. 21.3

Once I'm in here, I look at how each of the targeting groups have been performing over the past 30 days. I also look at how they have performed over a longer time period, such as *Lifetime* by clicking on the *Date range* drop-down menu.

	Active	Automatic targeting groups	Match type	Status	Suggested bid		Bid	Impressions	Clicks	CTR	⯆ Spend
		Total: 4			Apply all			12,170	80	0.66%	$37
	⬤	Loose match	-	Delivering	ⓘ $0.78 $0.71-$7.01	Apply	$ 0.33	6,813	52	0.76%	$26
	⬤	Close match	-	Delivering	ⓘ $0.56 $0.47-$0.67	Apply	$ 0.44	5,275	27	0.51%	$11
	◯	Substitutes	-	Paused Details ⯆	ⓘ $0.65 $0.46-$0.96	Apply	$ 0.12	82	1	1.22%	$0
	◯	Complements	-	Paused Details ⯆	ⓘ $0.59 $0.75-$0.77	Apply	$ 0.17	-	-	-	-

Go to page [1] < > 1 - 4 of 4 results   Results per page: 200 ⌄

Fig. 21.4

You can see from the screenshot above that I have already turned off the *Substitutes* and *Complements* targeting groups from this campaign because they weren't performing well.

Step 4

With each targeting group here, I'm looking for discrepancies between what each one has spent and what each one has generated in both *Sales* and *Estimated KENP royalties*.

	Active	Automatic targeting groups ⓘ		*Spend ⓘ	CPC ⓘ	Orders ⓘ	Sales ⓘ	ACOS ⓘ	KENP read ⓘ	Estimated KENP royalties ⓘ
☐		Total: 4	56%	$37.95	$0.47	19	$?.81	58.56%	7,046	$31.50
☐	⬤	Loose match ⓘ	76%	$26.44	$0.51	16	$55.84	47.35%	2,862	$12.80
☐	⬤	Close match ⓘ	51%	$11.39	$0.42	3	$8.97	126.98%	4,184	$18.71
☐	◯	Substitutes ⓘ	22%	$0.12	$0.12	-	-	-	-	-
☐	◯	Complements ⓘ	-	-	-	-	-	-	-	-

Go to page [1] ‹ › 1 - 4 of 4 results   Results per page: 200 ⌄

Fig. 21.5

If there is a discrepancy, I won't necessarily turn that targeting group off, unless, of course, the discrepancy is far beyond saving. Instead, I will reduce the bid of that targeting group.

If the targeting group is performing well, I may increase the bid by $0.05 – $0.10 to see if I can generate additional impressions and clicks and, hopefully, additional sales and page reads too.

I never want to increase the bid by $0.50 or $1.00 in one hit, because that is too much of a jump. Small, frequent changes with Amazon Ads are far better and easier to track than huge, infrequent changes.

Just keep in mind that the more impressions and clicks, the greater the risk of more wasted ad spend, so you will need to keep an eye on your search terms, which we'll be jumping into shortly, and nip these in the bud sooner rather than later.

IMPORTANT: When reducing bids on targeting groups, keywords, ASINs or categories, it's vital that you reduce the bid to a number that

is below the current cost per click (CPC). Otherwise, you will not see a reduction in cost for that target.

I like to use a bid that is below the CPC for that target based on the last 30 days of data; if I have already changed the bid within the last 30 days, I use the Last 7 days *to work out what my new bid will be.*

Step 5

Whilst I am in the targeting groups here, I'm also looking at which one, if any, is receiving the lion's share of the budget. You can usually figure this out relatively quickly by looking at the *Impressions* and the *Spend* columns.

	Active	Automi	Impressions	Clicks	CTR	Spend	CPC	Orders	Sales	ACOS	KENP read
		Total:	12,166	80	0.66%	$37.95	$0.47	19	$64.81	58.56%	7,046
		Loo... 55	6,812	52	0.76%	$26.44	$0.51	16	$55.84	47.35%	2,862
		Clo... 44	5,272	27	0.51%	$11.59	$0.42	3	$8.97	126.98%	4,184
		Sub ... 12	82	1	1.22%	$0.12	$0.12	-	-	-	-
		Co... 17	-	-	-	-	-	-	-	-	-

Go to page 1 < > 1 - 4 of 4 results   Results per page: 200 ∨

Fig. 21.6

If there is one targeting group that has considerably more impressions than the others, then, usually, it is also receiving the majority of the budget.

In these scenarios, what I sometimes do is turn off all the other targeting groups in this campaign, leaving active the one that has been receiving the most budget in this campaign. I will then create new campaigns for the other targeting groups, which allows them to receive enough budget to gather data.

Step 6

When I have reviewed each targeting group here and made any necessary adjustments to the bids, I will then look at the search terms for this ad group, by clicking on the *Search terms* option in the left-hand menu.

Fig. 21.7

Here, I'm looking for any search terms or ASINs that are receiving clicks (i.e., spending money) but not generating any sales or page reads, as I want to stop spending money on them as soon as possible.

Before starting this process, I change the *Date range* to the maximum possible: *Last 65 days*.

There are also some thresholds to keep in mind when running through this process. If a search term or ASIN has one click but no sales or page reads, I'm not immediately going to stop spending money on it.

I work to a threshold of 10-15 clicks, meaning that I am happy to spend *some* money on a search term or ASIN to give it a chance to prove itself as a worthy contender for scaling up.

So, I will let a search term or ASIN generate 10-15 clicks before I stop spending money on it. If there are no sales or page reads from it after it's had 10-15 clicks, then I will negate it using negative targeting, which we'll be going through shortly.

If I see a search term or ASIN that is completely irrelevant to the book I'm advertising, however, even if it's had just one click, I will negate it immediately; sometimes, using your common sense and your knowledge about your genre is more valuable than the data itself.

Step 7

When I come across a search term or ASIN that has had the 10-15 clicks, but no sales or page reads, or is completely irrelevant to the book I'm advertising, it's time to make use of negative targeting.

As you can see from the screenshot below, I have a search term here that has had 10 clicks, but no sales or page reads have been generated from it.

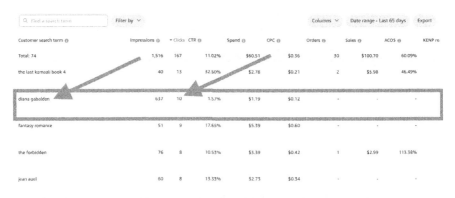

Fig. 21.8

So, I'm going to highlight this search term (*diana gabaldon*), right-click, and select *copy* (or Ctrl+C/Cmd+C).

Step 8

Next, select *Negative targeting* from the left-hand menu and click *Add negative keywords*.

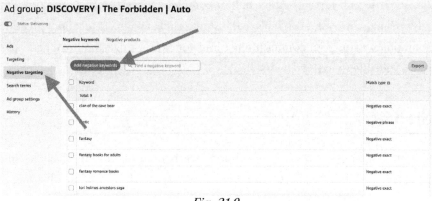

Fig. 21.9

Step 9

From here, paste the keyword for negating into the text box that pops up. In this instance, I'm going to add this as a *Negative exact* keyword. Once the keyword is in the text box, click *Add keywords* and then *Save*.

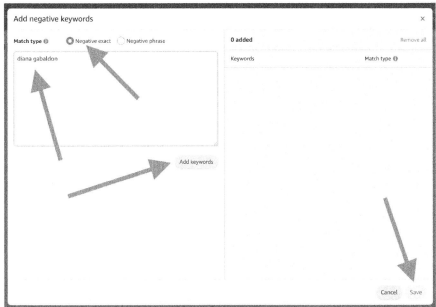

Fig. 21.10

Before we move on, I want to cover the differences between negative exact and negative phrase keywords, as they have very different uses and, without understanding them properly, by using the wrong one, you can quickly destroy a well-performing campaign.

Negative Exact Keywords

Using negative exact keywords will negate only that specific keyword and its plural or singular counterpart. For example, as we have just been through, negating the keyword *diana gabaldon* as a negative exact keyword will only negate that one keyword from triggering your ad to show.

If someone searches for *diana gabaldon outlander*, however, your ad can still be triggered to show, because the customer search query wasn't an exact replica of the keyword you are negating, *diana gabaldon*.

Negative Phrase Keywords

Now, taking the same example keyword, *diana gabaldon*, if we added this as a negative phrase keyword, this would wipe out any customer search query that included *diana gabaldon*, such as:

- *diana gabaldon books*
- *diana gabaldon outlander books*
- *diana gabaldon novels*
- *diana gabaldon books in order*

There are definitely situations where I use negative phrase keywords, but I generally use them for singular words that are either irrelevant or I have seen a trend of this one word wasting a lot of money. A negative phrase keyword will prevent your ad from triggering if that keyword is anywhere to be found within the customer search term.

For example, some common negative phrase keywords I add to ad groups include:

- *free* (don't use this if your book *is* free!)
- *audio*
- *audiobook*
- *audible*

So that is a brief overview of the important differences between negative exact and negative phrase keywords.

Step 10

If there are ASINs within your search terms that are irrelevant or have had 10-15 clicks but not generated any sales or page reads, you will need to add those as a negative product.

This option can be found in the same negative targeting section of the ad group that we've just been in, but instead of clicking *Negative keywords*, you select *Negative products*.

Fig. 21.11

Step 11

When you have found an ASIN to negate, copy that ASIN from the search terms table and come over to the *Negative products* section, then click the *Add negative product targets* button.

Fig. 21.12

Step 12

In the box that pops up, you can choose to:

- *Search* for the ASIN you want to negate
- *Enter* a list of ASINs you want to negate
- *Upload* a .csv file of the ASINs you want to negate

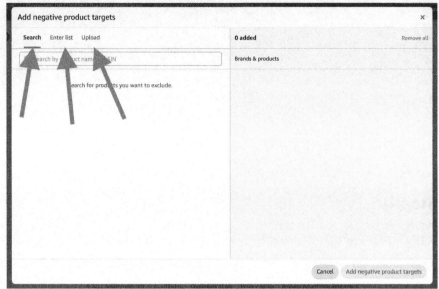

Fig. 21.13

When you're negating just one ASIN at a time, I prefer to use the *Search* option, by pasting the ASIN I've just copied from the search terms table into the search bar here.

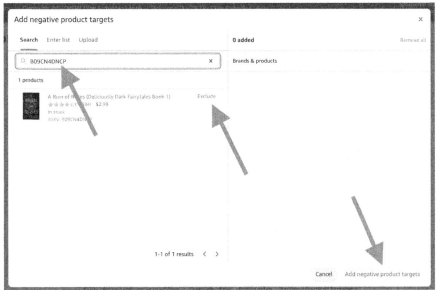

Fig. 21.14

Once you've entered the ASIN into the *Search* bar, hit the *Enter* key on your keyboard and then click the *Exclude* button, as highlighted above. Finally, click the button labeled *Add negative product targets* in the bottom right-hand corner of this box.

And that's it! You have successfully added an ASIN as a negative product target. From now on, your ad will not be shown on that ASIN's product page or associated placement relating to that ASIN.

Step 13

Once you have been through the search terms for this campaign and negated the required keywords and ASINs, head on back to the campaign settings by clicking the campaign name at the top of the page, as highlighted below.

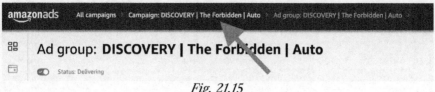

Fig. 21.15

Step 14

From here, we are going to look at the *Placements* option in the left-hand menu, to see where our ads are appearing and which *Placements* are performing best for us.

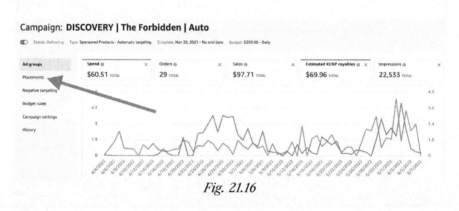

Fig. 21.16

Step 15

There are three possible *Placements* where your Amazon Ads can appear:

- *Top of search*
- *Product pages*
- *Rest of search*

Each of them is pretty self-explanatory, as I'm sure you can see!

Campaign: **DISCOVERY | The Forbidden | Auto**

Fig. 21.17

When looking at the performance of each placement, we can see the same metrics as we did when looking at individual keywords, ASINs and targeting groups, such as *Spend, CPC, CTR, Sales, Orders, KENP read, KENP royalties*, etc.

From this data, we can easily identify the best performing placements and make some adjustments; scratch that, just one adjustment, to two out of the three placements; *Top of search* and *Product pages*.

This is called the *Bid adjustment*.

With this option, we can tell Amazon to increase our base bid (i.e., the bid you set at the targeting group, keyword, ASIN, or category level) by a percentage of 1% – 900%.

We should only be using this option if a particular placement is performing well. Don't use it on a poor performing placement, otherwise you will just make a bad performer even worse!

If your base bid was $0.53, for example, and you saw that *Product pages* was your best performing placement, you could add a *Bid adjustment* to the *Product pages* placement.

Let's say we want to increase your bid for *Product pages* by 20%; this would change your maximum bid (for *Product pages* only) to $0.64. Your maximum bid for *Top of search* and *Rest of search* would remain at the base bid of $0.53.

You can see in the screenshot below that I have added a *100% Bid adjustment* to my *Top of search* placement for this automatic targeting campaign.

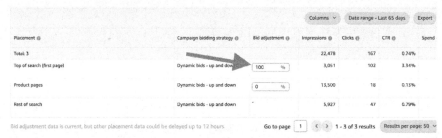

Placement ⓘ	Campaign bidding strategy ⓘ	Bid adjustment ⓘ	Impressions ⓘ	Clicks ⓘ	CTR ⓘ	Spend
Total: 3			22,478	167	0.74%	
Top of search (first page)	Dynamic bids - up and down	100 %	3,051	102	3.34%	
Product pages	Dynamic bids - up and down	0 %	13,500	18	0.13%	
Rest of search	Dynamic bids - up and down	-	5,927	47	0.79%	

Bid adjustment data is current, but other placement data could be delayed up to 12 hours.   Go to page [1] < > 1 - 3 of 3 results   Results per page: 50 ⌄

Fig. 21.18

Yes, this is fairly aggressive, but it is without doubt the best performing placement for this campaign, so I want to capitalize on it as much as possible. I could still push this *Bid adjustment* higher (up to 900%), but for the time being, I'm happy with where things are at.

So, review your *Placements*, figure out which is the best performer, and, if you feel confident enough, add a *Bid adjustment* to that best performer. You don't have to be as aggressive as I have been here with a *100% Bid adjustment*; start with 10% or 20% and assess the results.

One note about *Rest of search* placements ...

If *Rest of search* is your best performing placement, unfortunately, there is nothing you can do to influence that and capitalize on it further. All you can really do in this scenario is increase your base bid, but that will also increase your bid on *Product pages* and *Top of search*.

Step 16

The final stage of optimizing a campaign is adjusting the budget, if necessary.

To do this, click the *Ad groups* option in the left-hand menu and compare the total amount spent on this campaign over the past 30 days with how much it has generated in *Sales* and *Estimated KENP royalties*.

Fig. 21.19

If things are looking good and profitable for you (making sure you are looking at the big picture of your entire earnings for this book and/or series in your KDP dashboard), then increase your budget by heading over to the *Campaign settings* in the left-hand menu.

Fig. 21.20

You will then see an option to adjust your *Budget*, as highlighted in the screen-shot above.

I recommend you increase your budget gradually so as not to allow Amazon to run away with your money!

Unlikely as it is that Amazon will spend your entire daily budget in a day, it can and does happen – you have been warned. Having said this, as you can see from the above screenshot, this campaign has a daily budget of $250, and I'm lucky if it spends $5 in a single day!

Step 17

It's perfectly normal if some of your campaigns don't generate impressions or clicks, let alone sales or page reads, so don't despair as there are things you can do.

When I come across these under-performing (or non-performing) campaigns, as long as they've been running for at least 72 hours, I'll increase the bids on the targets within the campaign and see if that kicks things into gear. If that achieves little to nothing over the next three to four days, I'll increase the daily budget.

And if a budget increase doesn't get things moving, I'll change the bidding strategy from *Dynamic bids – down only* to *Fixed bids*, which you can do in the *Campaign settings* menu, as you can see below.

Fig. 21.21

If, after a month, the campaign is still not delivering, despite increasing the bids, daily budget, and adjusting the bidding strategy, I'll switch it off and re-create it from scratch because sometimes, despite everything, a campaign may just not work.

And that's it! I do this with all my campaigns once or twice per week, depending on the daily ad spend of the account.

Tomorrow is the final day, Day 7, where we will be protecting your author brand, an underrated, but highly important aspect of being successful with Amazon Ads, and on Amazon as a whole.

Action Step for Day 6

Optimize Your Campaigns

Once your campaigns have been running for at least a week or two, work through the steps we've covered here on Day 6 to optimize each of them.

If you only have a short amount of time for optimization, break it down to optimizing one campaign per day, which should take you five to ten minutes, depending on how much you are spending.

I optimize at the same time as picking out the keywords and ASINs I want to scale up into the performance phase campaigns, so feel free to do the same, or block out separate times/days for each task; design a workflow for managing your Amazon Ads that fits your schedule.

Day 7

Protecting Your Brand

B rand protection on Amazon is an underrated, underused strategy. Without it, though, you are potentially – no, let me rephrase that – you are *definitely* leaving money on the table.

So, today, the final day of this book, I'm going to walk you through what brand protection on Amazon is and how to set up your brand protection campaigns.

Chapter Twenty-two

What Is Brand Protection?

B rand protection will have different levels of success dependent on how prolific you are on Amazon.

If you are a brand-new author who released your first ever book last week, unless you're an A-list celebrity, you're not going to see big sales numbers from your brand protection campaigns immediately.

On the other hand, if you've been selling well on Amazon for six months or more, then brand protection campaigns can do wonders for your sales. The more prolific you are, the better these campaigns work.

What we are doing with brand protection campaigns is ensuring that whenever a reader searches for our books on Amazon, we are appearing right at the top of the search results.

When you start building a name for yourself on Amazon, you will find that other authors begin to target your author name and your books. If you're not protecting your brand, these authors can steal sales away from you, even if a reader was looking for your books, not theirs.

Take a look at the screenshot below, where you can see that I am protecting my wife's author name (Lori Holmes) through Amazon Ads.

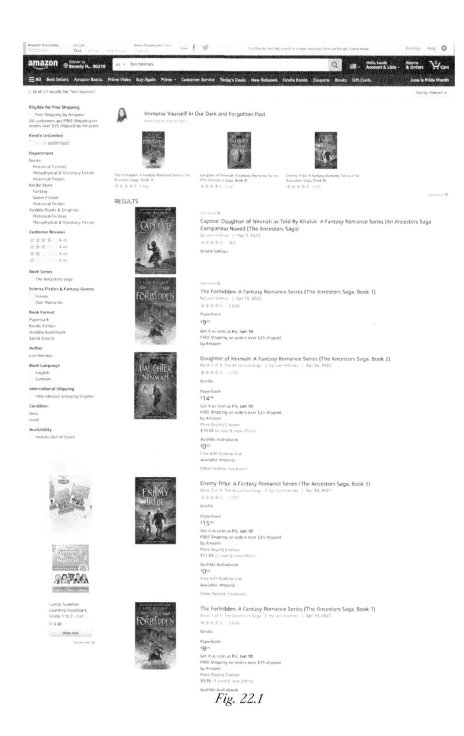

Fig. 22.1

There is a sponsored brands ad at the top of the page, followed by two sponsored products ads, followed further by multiple organic listings of Lori's books.

If I weren't running brand protection campaigns, other authors would have their books appearing in these sponsored brands and sponsored products placements on the search results page.

With these brand protection campaigns running, however, you can see that Lori's books are dominating the search results.

It's not just the search results where brand protection campaigns come into play though. Protecting your product pages is just as important, if not more so, than the search results pages, because the product pages are where readers make purchasing decisions.

There are so many other books available for readers to choose from when they are looking at your book product page; so many opportunities to be drawn away from your book towards someone else's.

This is where ASIN targeting comes into play.

As you already know from Day 4, with Amazon Ads, we can target specific ASINs. And this is exactly what we are doing with our brand protection campaigns: targeting our own books with our own books!

The more books you have in your catalog, the better this strategy will work.

The screenshot below is the sponsored products carousel on the product page for Book 1 of my wife's series; you can see that the first four books in the carousel here are other books in her series.

Sponsored @

Pre-order now

The Last Kamaali: A
Fantasy Romance Series
(The Ancestors Saga,
Book 4)
Lori Holmes
Kindle Edition
$2.99

Captive: Daughter of
Ninmah as Told By
Khalvir: A Fantasy
Romance Series (An...
Lori Holmes
★★★★☆ 365
Kindle Edition
$2.99

Enemy Tribe: A Fantasy
Romance Series (The
Ancestors Saga, Book 3)
Lori Holmes
★★★★☆ 1,334
Kindle Edition
$3.99

Daughter of Ninmah: A
Fantasy Romance Series
(The Ancestors Saga
Book 2)
Lori Holmes
★★★★☆ 1,191
Kindle Edition
$3.99

The Restaurant (The
Nantucket Restaurant
series Book 1)
Pamela M. Kelley
★★★★☆ 15,985
Kindle Edition
$4.99

Love Beyond Time (A
Scottish Time Travel
Romance): Book 1
(Morna's Legacy Series)
Bethany Claire
A lusty Scottish lord. A
time-traveling teacher. A
trick, history only she can
prevent. Can they change
fate and save their
impossible romance?
★★★★☆ 2,290
Kindle Edition
$0.00

The Forsaken King
Penelope Barsetti
★★★★☆ 1,672
Kindle Edition
$7.99

Fig. 22.2

There are currently, at the time of writing, five books in Lori's series. When there are more titles available, you can bet your bottom dollar I'll be adding them into this brand protection campaign!

Protecting your brand on Amazon, in my opinion, is a necessity and, without it, you are missing out on a lot of potential sales. These brand protection campaigns can be insanely profitable and, once they're setup, they take very little time and effort to manage.

So, let's dive in and launch these campaigns ...

Chapter Twenty-three

Launching Your Brand Protection Campaigns

Now you understand the importance of brand protection campaigns, let's dive right in and set them up. Here's what we're going to be launching together in this chapter:

- 1 x keyword targeting campaign [phrase match keywords]
- 1 x ASIN targeting campaign

First, before you launch any campaigns, you need to collect your ASINs and brand keywords, which you can do in the Amazon Ads Targeting Tool, included in the Amazon Ads Toolkit.

Inside, you'll find a tab titled *Brand ASINs and Brand KWs*. On this sheet, you'll see sections for your:

- Book titles
- ASINs of your Kindle books
- ISBNs of your print books
- Brand keywords

If you're struggling to know what to use as your brand keywords, here's what I recommend:

- Your author name
- Your book titles
- Your series titles

Once you've collected all your ASINs, ISBNs and brand keywords, it's time to launch ...

Brand Keyword Campaign Setup

We'll start by launching your brand keywords campaign ...

Step 1

As always, head on over to your Amazon Ads dashboard and click *Create campaign*.

Fig. 23.1

Step 2

Choose *Sponsored Products* when selecting a campaign type.

Fig. 23.2

Step 3

An important note about these brand keyword campaigns: I always add every book in the series I'm advertising into one ad group within the campaign. The reason being that I am including keywords that relate to specific books in the series.

You could make this campaign very granular by having one ad group for each book and only specific keywords in each ad group that relate to that book. From experience, however, any associated benefits (i.e., sales and page reads) you might get aren't worth the additional workload and management time.

So, select *Standard ad* and name this ad group. Here's how I name these brand campaigns:

BRAND | [SERIES TITLE] | Brand Keywords [PHRASE]

As an example, here's how this would look in reality:

BRAND | The Ancestors Saga | Brand Keywords [PHRASE]

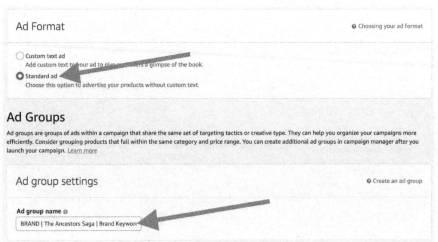

Fig. 23.3

As always, though, feel free to name your ad groups and campaigns in a format that works for you.

You'll also notice that I've included ***[PHRASE]*** in the ad group and campaign name; this is because we're only going to be targeting phrase match keywords in this campaign.

Once you have some data and know what brand keywords customers use when they're searching for your books, you can pull these keywords out from the search terms of this campaign (as we covered on Day 6) and create exact match keywords of those in a new campaign.

Step 4

Add all the books from this series that you're advertising, if applicable, into this campaign.

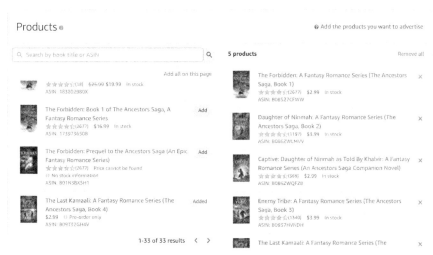

Fig. 23.4

Step 5

Next, choose *Manual targeting* and *Keyword targeting*.

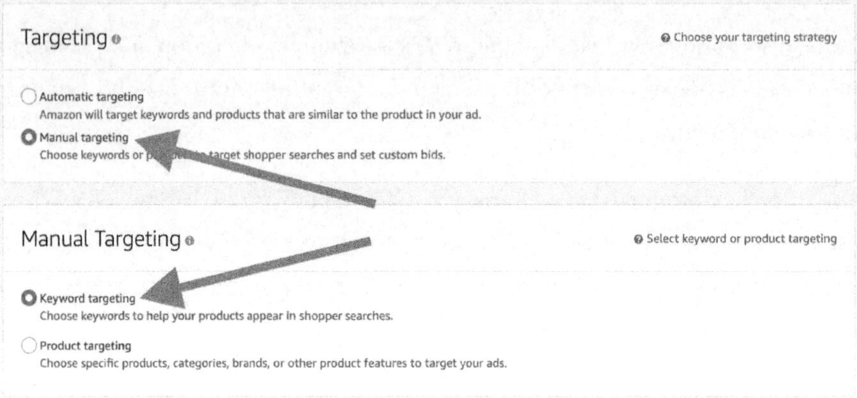

Fig. 23.5

Step 6

In the keyword targeting section, select the *Enter list* tab and de-select the *Broad* and *Exact* match type boxes, leaving just *Phrase* match checked. Enter a *Custom bid* of, I recommend, between $0.50 and $0.80. In this campaign, I'm going to set a bid of $0.78.

This may sound high, but as I've mentioned a few times throughout this book, Amazon loves and rewards *relevance*. You are clearly highly relevant to your own books, so Amazon will tend to reward you with lower cost per clicks (CPCs).

I have brand campaigns I'm running where my bid is $1.48 and my CPC is around $0.46; this is because the brand keywords I'm targeting are highly relevant to the author's books that I'm advertising.

Fig. 23.6

Step 7

Now it's time to enter your list of brand keywords into the text box. Once entered, click the *Add keywords* button.

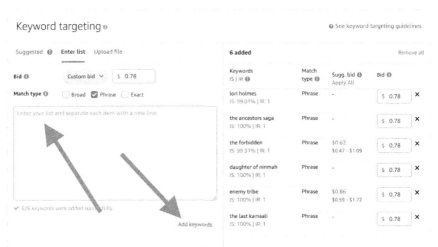

Fig. 23.7

Step 8

Next, scroll down the page, right past the negative targeting section, unless you know of any negative keywords you want to add, in which case, you can add those in now.

Typically, on a new brand keywords campaign, I leave all options open from the beginning and only negate irrelevant keywords when I see them in the data.

We'll continue down to the *Campaign bidding strategy* section where I select *Fixed bids* for brand keyword campaigns; I don't want Amazon to mess with my bids on these sorts of campaigns, so using *Fixed bids* ensures they take my full bid into consideration.

Fig. 23.8

Step 9

Copy and paste the ad group name you entered earlier into the *Campaign name* box on the campaign *Settings* section, then:

- Select your brand portfolio from the *Portfolio* drop-down
- Leave the *Start* and *End* date as default
- Choose a *Daily budget* (I recommend starting at $20 per day, but use a lower budget if that feels too high for you)

Fig. 23.9

Once you're happy with everything, click the *Launch campaign* button.

And that's it! You have just launched your first brand keywords campaign!

Your ads will soon start appearing in the search results when readers search for any of the keywords you've used in this campaign, as well as your organic listings. So, you will dominate the search results in no time!

Brand ASINs Campaign Setup

What about product pages, you ask? Let's move on to those now and protect your real estate on there as well.

Step 1

One more time ... head on over to your Amazon Ads dashboard and click *Create campaign*.

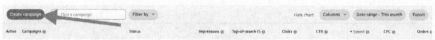

Fig. 23.10

Step 2

Choose the *Sponsored Products* option as the campaign type.

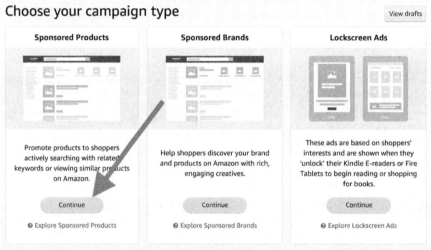

Fig. 23.11

Step 3

Select the *Standard ad* option as the ad format, but, differently from before, we're going to use a different naming convention for the *Ad group name* and the campaign name.

The reason for this is that we're going to have one campaign that houses multiple ad groups; one ad group per advertised book.

I name each ad group according to the title of that book and the order it comes in the series. For example, Book 1 of my wife's series is called *The Forbidden*, so I call this first ad group:

Book 1: The Forbidden

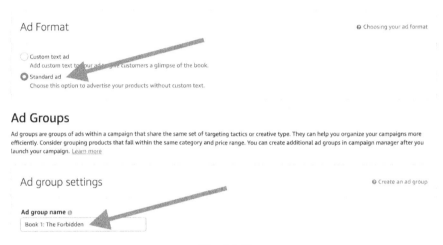

Fig. 23.12

Step 2

Select the first book in your series (or, if you write standalones, the first book you want to advertise in this campaign).

Fig. 23.13

Step 3

Next, select *Manual targeting* and then *Product targeting*.

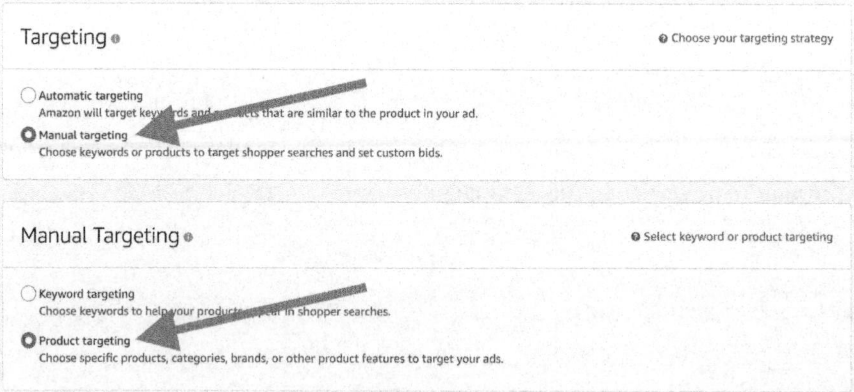

Fig. 23.14

Step 4

In the *Product targeting* section, click the *Individual products* tab.

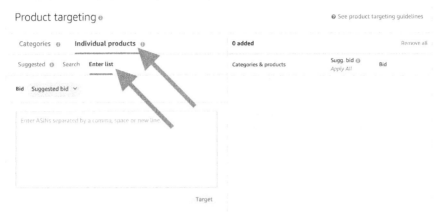

Fig. 23.15

Step 5

As with the brand keywords campaign, I like to have a high bid for the brand ASIN campaign too.

As ASINs are generally more expensive to target than keywords, I prefer to use a slighter higher bid than the brand keywords campaign. So, in this instance, I'll set a *Custom bid* of $0.88.

Fig. 23.16

Step 6

Now it's time to enter the ASINs of all your other books in this series, or other books in your catalog if you are advertising a standalone title.

So, select all the ASINs you want to target (making sure that you exclude the ASIN that you're advertising in this campaign), then copy and paste them to the text box and click the *Add target* button.

Also, ensure you are selecting the ASINs of the books that are the same format of the one you're advertising in this campaign. For example, if you're advertising the Kindle version of Book 1 of your series, the ASINs you're targeting here should be the ASINs of the Kindle versions, not the print versions. This may sound obvious, but it's very easily done!

We do this because we want to advertise our Kindle books to people who read Kindle books. And we want to advertise print books to people who prefer to read print books.

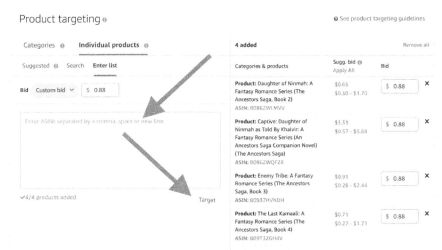

Product targeting ⓘ   ⦿ See product targeting guidelines

	Categories & products	Sugg. bid ⓘ Apply All	Bid
	Product: Daughter of Ninmah: A Fantasy Romance Series (The Ancestors Saga, Book 2) ASIN: B086ZWLMVV	$0.65 $0.30 - $1.70	$ 0.88 ✕
	Product: Captive: Daughter of Ninmah as Told By Khalvir: A Fantasy Romance Series (An Ancestors Saga Companion Novel) (The Ancestors Saga) ASIN: B086ZWQFZ8	$3.31 $0.57 - $5.68	$ 0.88 ✕
	Product: Enemy Tribe: A Fantasy Romance Series (The Ancestors Saga, Book 3) ASIN: B0937HVNDH	$0.91 $0.28 - $2.44	$ 0.88 ✕
	Product: The Last Kamaali: A Fantasy Romance Series (The Ancestors Saga, Book 4) ASIN: B09T32GH4V	$0.71 $0.27 - $1.71	$ 0.88 ✕

Fig. 23.17

To put all of this into context for you, in this first ad group, I'm advertising Book 1 of the series and targeting Books 2, 3, and 4 of the same series (as well as a companion novel to Book 2 of the series).

Step 7

There's no negative targeting to apply to this campaign, so we can scroll right on past that and change the *Campaign bidding strategy* to *Fixed bids*. Just as with the brand keywords campaign, I don't want Amazon messing around with my bid, so I use *Fixed bids* to gain complete control.

Fig. 23.18

Step 8

We're now moving on to the campaign *Settings*, and the first task here is to name the campaign. Here's how I name my brand ASIN campaigns:

BRAND | [SERIES NAME] | Self-Targeting ASINs

To put this into context ...

BRAND | The Ancestors Saga | Self-Targeting ASINs

As always, feel free to use your own naming convention if mine doesn't work for you.

Also on the campaign *Settings*:

- Add this campaign into your brand *Portfolio*
- Leave the *Start* and *End* date as default
- Enter your *Daily budget* (I like to start with $20 per day, but feel free to adjust accordingly)

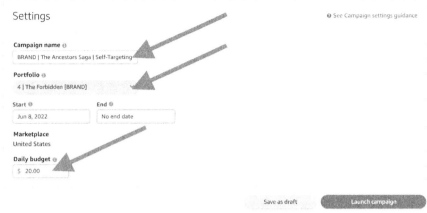

Fig. 23.19

When you're happy with everything, click the *Launch campaign* button.

Step 9

After launching your campaign, you will see an option in the bottom right of your screen called *Edit campaign*, highlighted below. Click this to go into the campaign *Settings*.

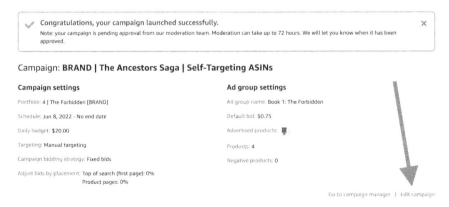

Fig. 23.20

Step 10

Once you're in the campaign *Settings*, click the *Ad groups* option on the left-hand menu.

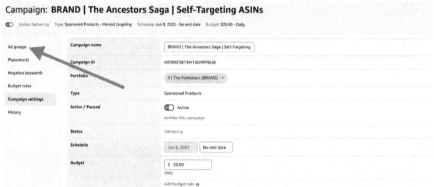

Fig. 23.21

Step 11

What we're going to do now is create a new ad group which is advertising, in this case, Book 2 of the series. To do this, scroll down the page a little and click the *Create ad group* button, highlighted below.

Fig. 23.22

Step 12

Name your ad group in the same format that you named the first ad group you created. Here's how I'm going to name this ad group:

Book 2: Daughter of Ninmah

Fig. 23.23

Step 13

Choose the relevant book to advertise in the *Products* section; I'm selecting Book 2 of the series here.

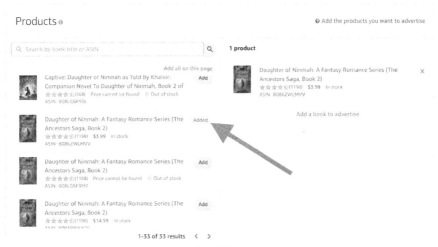

Fig. 23.24

Step 14

Scroll on down the page and you'll see that the *Campaign bidding strategy* is already set and can't be changed here. So, select *Product targeting* in the *Manual Targeting* section.

Fig. 23.25

Step 15

As before, select *Individual products* in the *Product targeting* section, then *Enter list* and set the same *Custom bid* as you did for the first ad group you created. For me, that bid is $0.88.

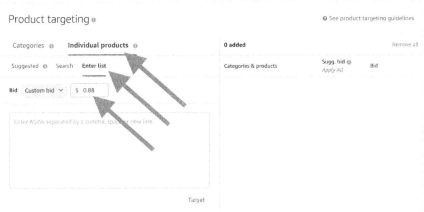

Fig. 23.26

Step 16

Next, copy and paste the relevant ASINs into the text box here and click the *Target* button. For me, when advertising Book 2 of the series, that means I'll be targeting the ASINs of:

- Book 1
- Book 3
- Book 4
- The companion novel

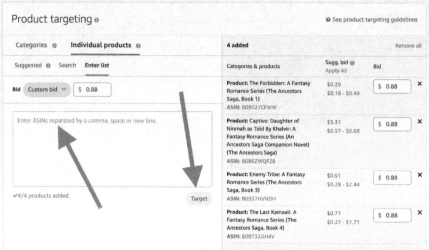

Fig. 23.27

Step 17

Finally, after a check through of all the details you've entered for this ad group, scroll to the bottom of the page, ignoring the negative targeting section, and click the *Create ad group* button.

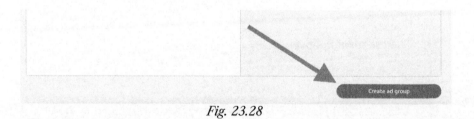

Fig. 23.28

Step 18

Now it's a case of rinse and repeat, creating the required number of ad groups within this campaign for your series or catalog of books.

Here's a rundown of what that looks like for me, which should help you create the right campaign and ad group structure for your books:

Ad Group 1

- **Advertising**: Book 1 of the series
- **Targeting**: Books 2, 3, 4, and the companion novel

Ad Group 2

- **Advertising**: Book 2 of the series
- **Targeting**: Books 1, 3, 4, and the companion novel

Ad Group 3

- **Advertising**: Book 3 of the series
- **Targeting**: Books 1, 2, 4, and the companion novel

Ad Group 4

- **Advertising**: Book 4 of the series
- **Targeting**: Books 1, 2, 3, and the companion novel

Ad Group 5

- **Advertising**: The companion novel
- **Targeting**: Books 1, 2, 3, and 4

And that, as they say in the movies, is a wrap!

You have one final Action Step to complete, and then, to tie a neat little bow on everything we've been through together over the past 7 days, I have some final thoughts and next steps for you to think about in the final section of this book, called Your Next Chapter. See you there!

Action Step for Day 7

Launch Your Brand Protection Campaigns

A s the final Action Step for this book, go ahead and follow the instructions in the last chapter to launch your two brand protection campaigns:

- 1 x keyword targeting campaign [phrase match]
- 1 x ASIN targeting campaign

Once launched, let these campaigns run indefinitely. Keep an eye on them, of course, but in the main, they take very little maintenance and can bring in very profitable sales and page reads for you.

Your Next Chapter

Well, you made it. You've reached the end of this book. Thank you, and well done for sticking with me all the way through.

Amazon Ads can be tricky to get moving, but once you get them dialed in, your sales, page reads (if you're in Kindle Unlimited), and bank balance will thank you.

There are so many ways you can use Amazon Ads, from launching a new book, promoting a pre-order, running them in the background as evergreen ads, revitalizing a book or series that has slipped into the telephone number rankings on Amazon, the possibilities are huge.

My aim with this book was to help authors, like yourself, to kick-start your Amazon Ads and start seeing results within weeks, not months or years.

The Amazon bookstore is a behemoth! It's difficult to make an impression and get the Amazon algorithm to take notice of your books without doing some form of paid advertising; relying on organic sales is becoming more and more difficult because of the sheer number of books on the platform.

Now, I'm not saying that organic sales aren't achievable; they most certainly are. And they can be amazing – who doesn't like book sales that you didn't have to pay for with ads! But you really need to be spending *some* money on advertising to *tickle* the Amazon algorithm enough for them to take notice and push your book organically.

Amazon Ads can do the *tickling* for you by increasing your sales and page reads, which improve your Amazon Best Seller Rank enough for the Amazon algorithm to take notice and move you into the top 100 of certain lists and categories. This brings more visibility to your books and generates sales and page reads *without* spending money on ads – these are the juicy organic sales that we love.

If I was to give you one big takeaway from this book, what would it be?

Test. And don't give up too soon.

Amazon Ads can be frustrating at times, either because they aren't generating any impressions or clicks, or because they won't scale, or they're spending money but you're not making it back through sales and page reads.

But remember this ...

Successful Amazon Ads come to those who wait. And test. And wait some more. And continue testing and tweaking.

Yes, Amazon Ads can be slow to gather data, but as I covered on Day 1, you really are playing the long game with Amazon Ads. So, take your time, dissect the data, and make strategic decisions from that data.

Amazon Ads aren't a silver bullet, but when you get them tuned in and refined, they make a big, no, a massive impact!

And remember the 80/20 rule because it is very prevalent within Amazon Ads. Most campaigns will work in some form or another, but only 20% of them will be absolute winners; put your attention (and budget) into these.

The same is true with your targeting; most keywords, ASINs, and categories won't do much for you, but the 20% that do ... nurture them. They are what will help you scale.

Stick with Amazon Ads, and they'll soon become your new best friend.

A little favor ... If you have found any form of value in this book, it would make my day if you could please leave an honest review and rating on Amazon to let other authors know what you thought of it.

Thank you so much. It's been a pleasure.

Yours,

Matthew J Holmes (Matt, for short!)

BONUS Action Step:

Download Your FREE Amazon Ads Toolkit

As I've mentioned before, learning without implementation is only going to get you so far; you need to take action to see momentum. As the saying goes, "An ounce of action is worth a tonne of theory."

And the more action you take, the more momentum you're going to see with your Amazon Ads and in your career as an author.

So, if you haven't done so already, make sure you download your FREE Amazon Ads Toolkit I've put together for you on the link below:

www.matthewjholmes.com/acos

About the Author

Advertising your books with Amazon Ads is simple, but it's not easy. Who doesn't love a challenge? I know I do, especially when it comes to advertising!

Whether you're brand new to Amazon Ads, a seasoned professional, or somewhere in between, my ultimate goal with all the content I share with authors is to provide you with a wealth of value, insights, and "ah-ah" moments.

To keep myself up to date with the latest opportunities, insights, ideas, strategies, and tactics, I offer hands-on Amazon Ads management for a select few authors. To find out more about working with me directly and to see if we are a good fit, please visit:

www.matthewjholmes.com/amazon-ads-management

On top of this, I also offer *Amazon Ads Group Coaching for Authors*, which includes monthly live coaching calls, Q&A sessions, and a thriving community of authors from around the world where we discuss all things Amazon Ads between our monthly coaching calls – check it out here:

www.matthewjholmes.com/coaching

If group coaching isn't for you, and you prefer to pace yourself, then my comprehensive *Amazon Ads Academy for Authors* course may be a better solution:

www.matthewjholmes.com/course

On a personal note, I live in England with my wife, Lori Holmes (www.matthewjholmes.com/lori), an author of fantasy novels, along with our three children, and two whippets, Freya and Loki.

When I'm not working, you can find me in our home gym, cycling, walking the dogs, spending time with my family, or getting out and about in the English countryside.

Printed in Great Britain
by Amazon

84822975R00127